Janet Raskin

READ THIS!

Fascinating Stories from the Content Areas

3

Alice Savage

With
Mary March
Jane Stanley McGrath
Lawrence J. Zwier

D1089344

CAMBRIDGE UNIVERSITY PRESS
Cambridge, New York, Melbourne, Madrid, Cape Town, Singapore,
São Paulo, Delhi, Dubai, Tokyo

Cambridge University Press
32 Avenue of the Americas, New York, NY 10013-2473, USA

www.cambridge.org
Information on this title: www.cambridge.org/9780521747936

First published 2010

Printed in Hong Kong, China, by Golden Cup Printing Company Limited

A catalog record for this publication is available from the British Library.

Library of Congress Cataloging-in-Publication Data

Savage, Alice, 1962-
  Read this! 3 : fascinating stories from the content areas / Alice Savage . . . [et al.].
    p. cm. — (Read this!)
  ISBN 978-0-521-74793-6 (pbk. : Student's bk.)
  1. English language — Textbooks for foreign speakers. 2. Interdisciplinary approach in education. I. Title.
II. Title: Fascinating stories from the content areas. III. Series.

  PE1128.S2797 2010
  428.6'4—dc22

2010003635

ISBN 978-0-521-74793-6 Student's Book
ISBN 978-0-521-74794-3 Teacher's Manual

Cambridge University Press has no responsibility for the persistence or
accuracy of URLs for external or third-party Internet Web sites referred to in
this publication, and does not guarantee that any content on such Web sites is,
or will remain, accurate or appropriate. Information regarding prices, travel
timetables, and other factual information given in this work are correct at
the time of first printing, but Cambridge University Press does not guarantee
the accuracy of such information thereafter.

Art direction, book design, layout services, and photo research: Adventure House, NYC
Audio production: Paul Ruben Productions

Contents

Introduction

ABOUT THE SERIES

Read This! is a three-level reading series for high beginning, low intermediate, and intermediate-level English learners. The series is designed to enhance students' confidence and enjoyment of reading in English, build their reading skills, and develop their vocabulary.

The readings in the series are high interest and content-rich. They are all nonfiction and contain fascinating true information. The style of writing makes the information easily digestible, and the language is carefully controlled at each level to make the texts just challenging enough, but easily accessible.

Each book in *Read This!* consists of five thematically related units. Each unit is loosely connected to a different academic discipline that might be studied in an institution of higher education, such as business, engineering, psychology, health care, or mathematics. Each unit is divided into three chapters, and each chapter contains a reading accompanied by exercise material. Besides the main theme of the unit, each chapter is tied to a secondary academic content area so that students can experience an interdisciplinary approach to a topic.

Accompanying each reading is a variety of pre- and postreading activities. They are designed to provide a balance of reading comprehension, vocabulary, and reading skill development. Many activities also provide opportunities for student discussion and a chance for students to connect the topics of the readings to their own lives and experience. Each unit ends with a wrap-up that reviews ideas and vocabulary from all three chapters of the unit.

Vocabulary instruction is an important focus of *Read This!* Selected words from each reading are previewed, presented, practiced, and recycled. These words are drawn from the two academic disciplines that are brought together in each reading. In addition, selected words from the Academic Word List (AWL) are pulled out from each reading for instruction.

Each unit is designed to take 6–9 hours of class time, depending on how much out-of-class work is assigned by the teacher. The units can either be taught in the order they appear or out of sequence. It is also possible to teach the chapters within a unit out of order. However, by teaching the units and chapters in sequence, students will benefit fully from the presentation, practice, and recycling of the target vocabulary.

All the readings in the *Read This!* series have been recorded for those students whose language learning can be enhanced by listening to a text as well as by reading it. However, since the goal of the series is to build students' readings skills, students should be told to read and study the texts without audio before they choose to listen to them.

The audio files can be found on the *Read This!* Web site at www.cambridge.org/readthis. Students can go to this site and listen to the audio recordings on their computers, or they can download the audio recordings onto their personal MP3 players to listen to them at any time.

An audio CD of the readings is also available in the back of each Teacher's Manual for those teachers who would like to bring the recorded readings into their classroom for students to hear. Also in the Teacher's Manual are photocopiable unit tests.

THE UNIT STRUCTURE

Unit Opener

The title, at the top of the first page of each unit, names the academic content area that unifies the three chapters in the unit. The title of each chapter also appears, along with a picture and a short blurb that hints at the content of the chapter reading. These elements are meant to intrigue readers and whet their appetites for what is to come. At the bottom of the page, the main academic content area of the unit is repeated, and the secondary academic content area for each chapter is given as well.

1 Topic Preview

The opening page of each chapter includes a picture and two tasks: Part A and Part B. Part A is usually a problem-solving task in which students are asked to bring some of their background knowledge or personal opinions to bear. Part B always consists of three discussion questions that draw students closer and closer to an idea of what the reading is about. In fact, the last question, *What do you think the reading is going to be about?* is always the same in every chapter: This is to help learners get into the habit of predicting what texts will be about before they read.

2 Vocabulary Preview

This section has students preview selected words that appear in the reading. It contains two tasks: Part A and Part B. Part A presents selected words for the students to study and learn. Part B has the students check their understanding of these words.

In Part A, the selected words are listed in three boxes. The box on the left contains words that relate to the main content area of the unit. The box on the right contains words that relate to the secondary content area of the reading. Between these two boxes are words from the reading that come from the Academic Word List (AWL). Placing the AWL words between the two lists of content area words creates a visual representation of the fact that the content area words are specific to separate content areas, while the AWL words are general academic words that might appear in either content area.

Note that the part of speech of a word is given in the chart only if this word could also be a different part of speech. Also note that some words are accompanied by words in parentheses. This alerts students to some common collocations that can form with the word and that will appear in the reading.

The vocabulary in the Vocabulary Preview is recycled over and over. The words appear in the reading; in Section 5, Vocabulary Check; in the Unit Wrap-Ups; and in the unit tests.

3 Reading

This section contains the reading and one or two pieces of art that illustrate it. Some words from the reading are glossed at the bottom of the page. These are low-frequency words that students are not expected to know. Understanding these words might be important for understanding the reading; however, it would probably not be useful for students to incorporate the words into their active vocabulary.

The icon at the top of the page indicates that the reading is available as an MP3 file online. Students can access this by going to the *Read This!* Web site at www.cambridge.org/readthis.

4 Reading Check

This section is designed to check students' comprehension of the text. Part A checks their understanding of the main ideas. Part B asks students to retrieve more detailed information from the reading.

5 Vocabulary Check

In this section, students revisit the same vocabulary that they studied before they read the text and that they have since encountered in the reading. The Vocabulary Check contains two tasks: Part A and Part B. In Part A, students are asked to complete a text by choosing appropriate vocabulary words for the context. The text in Part A is essentially a summary of the most salient information in the reading. This activity both reinforces the target vocabulary for the chapter and the content of the reading.

Part B varies from chapter to chapter. Sometimes it has a game-like quality, where students have to unscramble a word or find the odd word out in a group of words. Sometimes the task helps students extend their understanding of the target words by working with other parts of speech derived from the words. Other times, the task tests students' knowledge of other words that the target words often co-occur with (their collocations).

6 Applying Reading Skills

An important strand of *Read This!* is reading skill development. Students are introduced to a variety of skills, such as finding main ideas and supporting details, inferencing, identifying cause and effect, and organizing information from a reading into a chart. Practicing these skills will help students gain a deeper understanding of the content of the reading and the author's purpose. The section opens with a brief explanation of the reading skill and why it is important.

This section has two tasks: Part A and Part B. In Part A, students usually work with some kind of graphic organizer that helps them practice the skill and organize information. This work will prepare them to complete Part B.

7 Discussion

This section contains at least three questions that will promote engaging discussion and encourage students to connect the ideas and information in the readings to their own knowledge and experience. Many of the questions take students beyond the readings. There is also ample opportunity for students to express their opinions. This section helps students consolidate their understanding of the reading and use the target vocabulary from the chapter.

WRAP-UP

Each unit ends with a Wrap-Up, which gives students the chance to review vocabulary and ideas from the unit. It will also help them prepare for the unit test. (The photocopiable unit tests are to be found in the Teacher's Manual.) Teachers may want to pick and choose which parts of the Wrap-Up they decide to have students do, since to do all the activities for every unit might be overly time-consuming. The Wrap-Up section consists of the following:

Vocabulary Review. All the target vocabulary from the three chapters of the unit is presented in a chart. The chart is followed by an activity in which students match definitions to some of the words in the chart.

Vocabulary in Use. Students engage in mini-discussions in which they use some of the target language from the unit. Students will be able to draw on their personal experience and knowledge of the world.

Role Play. Students work with the concepts of the readings by participating in a structured and imaginative oral activity. The role plays require that the students have understood and digested the content of at least one of the readings in a chapter. One advantage of role plays is that they are self-leveling. In other words, the sophistication of the role play is determined by the level and oral proficiency of the students. Students will need help in preparing for the role plays. They will also need time to prepare for them. It might be a good idea for the teacher to model the first role play with one of the stronger students in the class.

Writing. This section of the Wrap-Up provides the teacher with an opportunity to have students do some writing about the content of the unit. The setup of this section varies from unit to unit.

WebQuest. For those students, programs, or classrooms that have Internet access, students can log onto www.cambridge.org/readthis. They can then find the WebQuest for the unit that they have been studying. The WebQuest is essentially an Internet scavenger hunt in which students retrieve information from Web sites that they are sent to. In this way, students encounter the information from the chapters once more. The Web sites confirm what they have already read and then broaden their knowledge of the unit topics by leading them to additional information. The WebQuests may be done individually or in pairs. Students may either submit their answers to the teacher online or they can print out a completed answer sheet and hand it in to the teacher.

Acknowledgments

Many people have been involved in the development, writing, and editing of *Read This! 3*. I would especially like to thank Bernard Seal for bringing me into the project. His involvement in the series and his knowledge of the field have helped at every step.

I was happy to have the opportunity to work with the talented writers Mary March, Jane McGrath, and Lawrence Zwier. My editor, Karen McAlister Shimoda, and managing editor, Kathleen O'Reilly, have done an outstanding job of keeping me on track. Thanks, too, to the production editor, Katharine Spencer; the copyeditor, Sylvia Bloch; and the fact checker, Mandie Drucker.

I am grateful to the reviewers, whose comments and suggestions were most helpful: John Bunting, Georgia State University; Mohammed Etedali, Kuwait; Devra Miller, San Mateo Unified High School District; Wendy Ramer, Broward Community College; Hsin Yi Shen, Taiwan; and Kerry Vrabel, Gateway Community College.

Special thanks go to Averil Coxhead for permission to cite from the Academic Word List (AWL). For the most up-to-date information on the AWL, go to: http://www.victoria.ac.nz/lals/resources/academicwordlist.

I would like to thank my colleagues at Lone Star College System: Dr. Head, Dr. Brock, and Dr. Harrison. You make Lone Star North Harris a great place to work. David, Pat, Sharilyn, Gwen, Katie, Janice, and Colin: you are the best. And of course I want to thank the students. You have been so much fun and taught me so much that I hardly consider it work.

I would also like to thank my family: Masoud, Cyrus, and Kaveh. You make home a great place to play!

Alice Savage

UNIT 1

Tourism and Hospitality

Chapter 1

Ice Hotel

A newly married couple goes on a memorable vacation.

Content areas:
- Tourism and Hospitality
- Art

Chapter 2

The Traveling Chef

A chef who travels around the world has an interesting way to learn about cultures.

Content areas:
- Tourism and Hospitality
- Culinary Arts

Chapter 3

Sail High in the Sky

One of the tallest and most luxurious hotels in the world looks like a sail in the sky.

Content areas:
- Tourism and Hospitality
- Engineering

1

Ice Hotel

1 TOPIC PREVIEW

A If you were going to stay at a hotel, what would be most important to you? Put your choices in order from 1 to 6, with 1 being your first choice. Share your answers with your classmates.

_____ a comfortable bed

_____ a restaurant with good food

_____ a large room

_____ a fitness center

_____ a quiet room

_____ _____ (your idea)

B Read the title of this chapter, look at the picture, and discuss the following questions.

1 Where do you stay when you travel? At a hotel? At a family member's house? At a friend's house? Explain.

2 What do you think an ice hotel might be like? Explain.

3 What do you think the reading is going to be about?

2 VOCABULARY PREVIEW

A Read the word lists. Put a check (✓) next to the words that you know and can use in a sentence. Compare your answers with a partner. Then look up any unfamiliar words in a dictionary.

Tourism and Hospitality	Academic Word List	Art
book (v.) check in (v.) destination (take an) excursion pack (v.) (luxury) suite	appreciate approach (v.) construct predict unique	architect carve gallery sculpture

The chart shows selected words from the reading related to tourism and hospitality, art, and the Academic Word List (AWL). For more information about the AWL, see page 121.

B Fill in the blanks with words from Part A.

1 It can take a lot of planning to choose a vacation _____ .

2 As you _____ the building, look at the flowers near the door.

3 Some artists like to _____ shapes out of wood.

4 Don't forget to _____ warm clothes for your winter trip.

5 Her artwork is _____ . I've never seen anything like it before.

6 After we _____ at the front desk, we can go to our room.

7 A/an _____ was hired to plan a new office building.

8 It is nice, but expensive, to stay in a/an _____ at a hotel.

9 They planned to _____ a new hotel to replace the old one.

10 The new art _____ has some famous paintings.

11 It is difficult to _____ the weather.

12 The family is going to take a/an _____ to the mountains.

13 When are you going to _____ your trip to London?

14 Hotel guests _____ comfortable beds and quiet rooms.

15 On their trip, they bought a/an _____ of a bird made of stone.

Preview the questions in Reading Check Part A on page 6. Then read the story.

Ice Hotel

The aurora borealis

1   Close to the Arctic Circle in Finnish Lapland,[1] there is a castle made of ice. It shines with blue light in the late winter afternoon. It looks like it could be the home of an ice princess in a fairy tale.[2] The walls are blocks of snow, and ice sculptures in the form of sea creatures guard the entrance. A honeymoon[3] couple, Paul and Karen Anderson, approach the entrance. As they walk to the front door, they hear the crunch of their boots on the snow and see the twinkle of stars in the sky, even though it is only four o'clock in the afternoon. They step inside the castle, hoping for a unique experience to remember.

2   The Andersons are among a growing number of tourists who are looking for an unusual vacation destination. They are about to stay at the Snow Castle in Kemi – a hotel shaped like a castle and made of ice! Ice hotels are becoming more common to find in the coldest regions of the world. Architects, engineers, and builders construct the hotels from the first ice and snow of winter. Each spring the castles melt, and each winter they are completely rebuilt.

---

[1] *Lapland:* a region near the Arctic Circle that includes the northern parts of Sweden, Finland, Norway, and Russia

[2] *fairy tale:* a story for children, usually with magic in it and a happy ending

[3] *honeymoon:* a vacation taken by two people who have just married

Karen and Paul have chosen to stay at this particular hotel in the far north of Finland because it is famous for its ice sculptures. They have also come to appreciate the unique beauty of the Arctic winter. The temperatures can go as low as -20° Fahrenheit (-29° Celsius), but Paul and Karen have packed their warmest clothes and they are ready. 3

Although the sun never rises above the horizon in midwinter, the daytime sky is not as black as the night. Instead, it is a dark bluish-gray. Lucky people might even see the blue, green, red, and white northern lights that dance across the sky. These northern lights, called the *aurora borealis*, happen about 200 times during the winter months. However, it is impossible to predict when they will appear. 4

Karen and Paul walk slowly through the castle. Before checking in, they tour the art gallery and admire the sparkling ice sculptures with colorful lights shining inside them. There are sculptures of boats, fish, and waves that remind them of their summer vacations. However, they can't imagine wearing their beach clothes here because the temperature inside the hotel is only 23° Fahrenheit (-5° Celsius). Then, they leave the art gallery and go to the restaurant where the tables and chairs are all carved out of ice. They try reindeer[4] soup with bread. The soup is hot and delicious and warms them up. 5

After dinner, Paul and Karen go to their room. They have booked the luxury suite. It is a large, comfortable room, with soft blue and green lights shining inside starfish and mermaid[5] sculptures. The bed, which is also made of ice, is covered with animal skins. The couple stays warm in their sleeping bags on top of the bed. 6

The next day, Karen and Paul take an excursion on an icebreaker, a ship that cuts through heavy ice. The three-hour tour on the ship includes a stop to go ice swimming. Some passengers, including the Andersons, put on special wet suits to keep them warm. Then they jump into the freezing water through a hole in the ice. 7

On their final night, Paul and Karen take turns driving a team of dogs on a dogsled. On the way back through the snowy forest, they look up at the sky and observe the dancing colors of the aurora borealis. What a special way for them to end this memorable honeymoon. 8

---

[4] *reindeer:* a type of deer that has horns like tree branches and lives in colder, northern parts of the world

[5] *mermaid:* an imaginary creature with the upper body of a woman and the tail of a fish

4 READING CHECK

A Circle the letter of the best answer.

1 Why are more and more tourists choosing to stay at an ice hotel?
  a They don't like warm-weather vacations.
  b They are looking for unusual vacation experiences.
  c They love ice sculptures.

2 What is the Snow Castle in Kemi?
  a an ice hotel only for newly married couples
  b an ice hotel that was once owned by a princess
  c an ice hotel in Finnish Lapland

3 When do people visit the Snow Castle?
  a in the winter only
  b in the winter and spring
  c in the summer, winter, and spring

B Are these statements true or false? Write *T* (true) or *F* (false).

1 _____ Paul and Karen are on their honeymoon.

2 _____ The Snow Castle in Kemi is the only snow castle in the world.

3 _____ When the Andersons arrived in Kemi, it was dark at 4 p.m.

4 _____ The ice hotel melts in the spring.

5 _____ Karen and Paul packed beach clothes.

6 _____ In the middle of winter in Kemi, the sun never rises above the horizon.

7 _____ The aurora borealis happens about 400 times in the winter.

8 _____ There are no lights inside the castle.

9 _____ The tables and chairs in the restaurant are carved out of ice.

10 _____ The reindeer soup is served cold.

11 _____ There are no ice sculptures in the suites.

12 _____ The Andersons went ice swimming.

5 VOCABULARY CHECK

A Retell the story. Fill in the blanks with the correct words from the box.

appreciate	approached	architects	booked	checked in
construct	excursion	gallery	predict	suite

Paul and Karen Anderson decided to go to Finnish Lapland for their honeymoon. They both _____ art, and they learned that the Snow Castle in Kemi, Finland, is famous for its artistic design and its beautiful art _____. They also learned that the Snow Castle is made of ice! The castle melts in the spring, but _____, engineers, and builders _____ it again every winter.

Paul and Karen _____ the luxury _____, but before they _____, they toured the castle. The next day, they took a/an _____ on an icebreaker and went ice swimming.

When the couple _____ the entrance to the Snow Castle on the first day, they looked up at the stars in the sky. They knew that you can't _____ when the aurora borealis will appear. However, on their last night, they had a lucky experience – they finally saw the beautiful northern lights.

B Write a short advertisement for the Snow Castle in Kemi. Use the following words: *destination, carve, sculptures, pack,* and *unique.*

_____

_____

_____

_____

_____

_____

_____

6 APPLYING READING SKILLS

> **Understanding the order of events** *in a reading means that you know what happens first, second, third, and so on. Making a time line is an excellent way to help you keep track of the order of events.*

A Write the letter of the following events into the time line in the correct order.

Paul and Karen . . .
a went to their room.
b toured the art gallery.
c drove a dogsled.
d saw the aurora borealis.
e took an excursion on an icebreaker.
f arrived at the Snow Castle.
g ate in the restaurant.

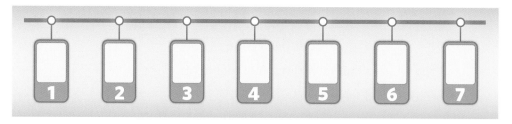

B Circle the correct word for each sentence about Paul and Karen Anderson's honeymoon. Use information from your time line in Part A.

1 They took an excursion on an icebreaker (before / after) they went on a dogsled.

2 They went to their room (before / after) they toured the art gallery.

3 They saw the aurora borealis (before / after) they arrived at the Snow Castle.

4 They ate in the restaurant (before / after) they went to their room.

7 DISCUSSION

Discuss the following questions in pairs or groups.

1 Do you think an ice hotel would be a comfortable place to stay? Explain.
2 Do you know of any other unique hotels? Explain.
3 If you could go to an unusual vacation destination, where would you go?

CHAPTER

2

The Traveling Chef

Courtesy of The Travel Channel, L.L.C.

1 TOPIC PREVIEW

A What do you like to do when you travel? Put a check (✓) next to your answers. Share your answers with your classmates.

1 _____ visit museums

2 _____ go on organized sightseeing tours

3 _____ relax on a beach

4 _____ eat local food

5 _____ meet local people

6 _____ _____ (your idea)

B Read the title of this chapter, look at the picture, and discuss the following questions.

1 When you travel, are you careful about what you eat and drink? Explain.

2 Do you recognize any of the food in the picture? Is it unusual to you? What is the most unusual food you have ever eaten?

3 What do you think the reading is going to be about?

2 VOCABULARY PREVIEW

A Read the word lists. Put a check (✓) next to the words that you know and can use in a sentence. Compare your answers with a partner. Then look up any unfamiliar words in a dictionary.

Tourism and Hospitality	Academic Word List	Culinary Arts
guide (*n.*)	distinct	beverage
museum	diverse	cuisine
scenery	interaction	fried
souvenir	reluctant	recipe
	significant	spice
	traditional	

The chart shows selected words from the reading related to tourism and hospitality, culinary arts, and the Academic Word List (AWL). For more information about the AWL, see page 121.

B Write the word from Part A next to its definition.

 1 A drink of any type: _____

 2 The natural things you see in the countryside: _____

 3 Instructions for cooking a particular food: _____

 4 Cooked in hot oil or fat: _____

 5 Very important: _____

 6 Communication with someone: _____

 7 A person whose job it is to show a place to visitors: _____

 8 Clearly different from others; special: _____

 9 A building with valuable or interesting objects: _____

 10 Something you keep to remind you of a special place: _____

 11 A flavoring for food: _____

 12 Following the customs or beliefs from the past: _____

 13 Different or varied: _____

 14 Not wanting to do something: _____

 15 A style of cooking: _____

MP3 **3** READING

Preview the questions in Reading Check Part A on page 13. Then read the story.

The Traveling Chef

Courtesy of The Travel Channel, L.L.C.

Andrew Zimmern in Ethiopia

What do you usually do when you travel? Visit museums? Take   1
pictures of mountains and other beautiful scenery? Relax on a beach?
Not Andrew Zimmern. His passion is to learn about new cultures
by exploring their cuisine. On his travels, he spends his time eating
local food and drinking local beverages with the people who live in the
area. He will eat almost anything: Jellyfish[1] salad, fried caterpillars,[2]
pickled[3] snake heads – anything. He will eat whatever his hosts offer
him. Some people are reluctant to try food that is different from what
they're used to. Not Zimmern. Grasshopper[4] pie? Why not? How about
bacon-and-eggs ice cream? Sure! He'll try it.

Andrew Zimmern is a chef, food writer, and host of an American   2
television travel program. On his show, he teaches his audience that
sharing food with people from other cultures is a great way to build
relationships with them, even if they don't speak your language. He
explains that there are rules about eating in different cultures that
are important to know. For example, in some cultures, it is polite to
make a noise while you are eating; in others, you should eat as quietly

---

[1] *jellyfish:* a sea animal with a soft, round body that can almost be seen through

[2] *caterpillar:* a small animal with a narrow body and many legs that grows into a
butterfly

[3] *pickled:* in a liquid containing salt or vinegar

[4] *grasshopper:* an insect that has long back legs, making it able to jump high

as possible. He also explains to his audience that in some cultures, you should eat everything your host offers you – even when you hate it – while in others, it is actually polite to leave food on your plate.

3   Africa is one of Zimmern's favorite places to travel. On one of his recent trips, he went to Tanzania, the largest country in East Africa. He traveled to northern Tanzania, where the Maasai tribe lives. His guide was a tall, thin Maasai man dressed in a traditional red cloth. Zimmern and his guide didn't speak the same language, but they laughed together as Zimmern participated in the Maasai tradition of drinking fresh cow's blood mixed with milk. For the Maasai, cows are a valuable part of their lives, providing them with almost everything they need to survive. Maasai men believe that drinking the blood from cows gives them strength.

4   When Zimmern visited Ethiopia, located in the Horn of Africa, he visited a butcher shop. There, he ate freshly killed raw camel meat, which local people eat on special occasions. Even without a common language, the men working in the shop had big smiles on their faces when they looked at Zimmern eating. He obviously loved the raw meat, which was dipped in lemon and spices.

5   The smell of fresh-roasted coffee fills the villages in Ethiopia. Ethiopian coffee is famous around the world, and Ethiopians are proud that the region called "Kaffee" is the birthplace of coffee. Drinking coffee is a significant part of the daily life of Ethiopians. In fact, every day when friends or family visit, they have coffee ceremonies that can last up to three hours! The ceremony starts with washing and roasting the beans, followed by serving the coffee in small cups without handles. The distinct smell fills the room as the guests talk and laugh. Zimmern drank three cups of coffee in a ceremony because it's not considered polite to drink only one or two. He was pleased to take part in this traditional form of hospitality.

6   Andrew Zimmern doesn't return home with pictures of buildings, waterfalls, or wildlife from his many trips. He comes home with souvenirs that are much more valuable to him: memories and videos of his interactions with the people from the diverse places he visits. Of course, he also brings back food and recipes. Every time he prepares food that he learned about in his travels, he remembers the people and places where he first experienced the food. He gets great pleasure in sharing his knowledge, recipes, and stories with his readers and television audience.

4 READING CHECK

A Are these statements true or false? Write *T* (true) or *F* (false).

1 _____ Andrew Zimmern believes in meeting local people when he travels.

2 _____ Andrew Zimmern eats only food that he knows he likes.

3 _____ Andrew Zimmern doesn't like to travel, but he has to for his job.

B Answer the questions with information from the reading.

1 What type of job does Zimmern have? Explain.

_____

2 How does Zimmern like to learn about new cultures?

_____

3 What are two examples of things Zimmern explains to his audience?

_____

4 What continent does Zimmern especially like to visit?

_____

5 Whom did Zimmern meet in Tanzania? What did they do together?

_____

6 Where did Zimmern eat raw camel meat?

_____

7 Why did Zimmern drink three cups of coffee in Ethiopia?

_____

8 What does Zimmern bring home from his travels?

_____

5 VOCABULARY CHECK

A Retell the story. Fill in the blanks with the correct words from the box.

beverage	cuisines	diverse	fried	guide
museums	recipes	reluctant	significant	souvenirs

Andrew Zimmern is not _____ to try unusual food. In fact, he

₁

learns about _____ cultures through their _____ .

₂ ₃

He has tried everything from eating _____ caterpillars to

₄

drinking a _____ with blood. Traveling and eating different

₅

foods are _____ parts of his life.

₆

When Zimmern traveled to Africa, in Tanzania his _____

₇

was a man that communicated with him through laughing and sharing

a special drink. In Ethiopia, he ate raw meat and drank coffee with

local people.

Zimmern doesn't visit _____ when he travels. He prefers to

₈

bring back _____ and _____ that remind him of

₉ ₁₀

the people he met and the food that he ate.

B Fill in the blanks with the correct words. Do not use more than one form of each word.

Noun	Adjective	Adverb
distinction	distinct	distinctly
interaction	interactive	–
scenery	scenic	–
spice	spicy	–
tradition	traditional	traditionally

1 There are _____ differences between those two countries.

2 Let's take the _____ route when we drive to our destination.

3 There was good _____ between the local people and the guests.

4 _____ , brides in China wear red at their wedding ceremony.

5 Korean and Thai food is _____ but delicious.

6 APPLYING READING SKILLS

> *Finding main ideas and supporting details* in a reading is an important skill.
> First, readers usually find the main ideas. Then good readers also look for
> details that support the main ideas.

A Write *M* next to the two sentences that are main ideas. Write *S* next to the
sentences that give supporting details. Match the *S* sentences to the *M*
sentences they support.

1 _____ He learned about a Maasai tradition of drinking cow's blood.

2 _____ When traveling, Andrew Zimmern likes to eat local food with
local people.

3 _____ Some people are reluctant to try food that is new to them.

4 _____ He will eat fried caterpillars and grasshopper pie.

5 _____ Andrew Zimmern likes to learn about new cultures when he travels.

6 _____ He will eat almost anything.

B Find two details from the text that support each main idea.

MAIN IDEA	SUPPORTING DETAILS
1 Africa is one of Andrew Zimmern's favorite places to travel.	
2 Andrew Zimmern explains different cultural customs about eating to his television audience.	
3 Andrew Zimmern comes home with valuable souvenirs of his trips.	

7 DISCUSSION

Discuss the following questions in pairs or groups.

1 Would you be able to try all the foods Andrew Zimmern has
tried? Explain.

2 What do you think are the most unusual foods in your culture?

3 If people from a different culture came to your house for a meal, what
would you tell them about your customs in food and eating?

CHAPTER
3
Sail High in the Sky

1 TOPIC PREVIEW

A Which of these locations do you think would be the most interesting places for a hotel? Put your choices in order from 1 to 6, with 1 being your first choice. Share your answers with your classmates.

_____ under the water

_____ on a small tropical island in the middle of the ocean

_____ on a ship that sails around the world

_____ on the top of a very high mountain

_____ in the middle of a large shopping mall

_____ _____ (your idea)

B Read the title of this chapter, look at the picture, and discuss the following questions.

1 Have you ever seen an unusual-looking building? Explain.
2 Describe the picture. Where do you think it was photographed?
3 What do you think the reading is going to be about?

2 VOCABULARY PREVIEW

A Read the word lists. Put a check (✓) next to the words that you know and can use in a sentence. Compare your answers with a partner. Then look up any unfamiliar words in a dictionary.

Tourism and Hospitality	Academic Word List	Engineering
amenities chauffeur concierge greet limousine	challenge (n.) design (v.) foundation layer (n.) project (n.) structure (n.)	concrete (n.) exterior facade support (v.)

The chart shows selected words from the reading related to tourism and hospitality, engineering, and the Academic Word List (AWL). For more information about the AWL, see page 121.

B Fill in the blanks with words from Part A.

1 They decided to make the outside stairs out of _____ .

2 Someone will _____ you when you arrive at the airport.

3 The _____ for that new school being built is very deep.

4 Which architect is going to _____ the hotel?

5 It is a/an _____ to build tall, safe buildings.

6 They took a/an _____ from the airport to their hotel.

7 The _____ took five years to complete.

8 Many hotels have _____ like room service and fitness centers.

9 The _____ of the building is painted white; the interior is blue.

10 Many hotels have a/an _____ who will help guests.

11 Strong walls are needed to _____ the building.

12 The bridge is the longest _____ in the world.

13 The _____ drove them all around the city.

14 As you approach the hotel, notice its beautiful _____ .

15 There is a/an _____ of stone under the dirt.

3 READING

Preview the questions in Reading Check Part A on page 20. Then read the story.

Sail High in the Sky

A suite at the Burj Al Arab

1   As you look out your airplane window and approach Dubai, the Persian Gulf twinkles in the sun. Something catches your eye. It's a large building on the water, but it looks like a white sail blowing in the wind. This sail, you quickly realize, is where you'll be staying during your visit to Dubai in the United Arab Emirates. You've climbed the stairs to the top of the Eiffel Tower in Paris, France. You've walked across the bridge connecting the Petronas Twin Towers in Kuala Lumpur, Malaysia. Now you'll be sleeping in one of the most architecturally unique hotels in the world, the Burj Al Arab, or "Arabian Tower."

2   After you land at the Dubai airport, a hotel representative greets you. Then she takes you to a Rolls-Royce limousine. After your long flight, you feel refreshed when the chauffeur presents you with a rose and a cold towel. This is the beginning of the exceptional service you'll experience throughout your stay at the Burj Al Arab. As the limousine crosses a private bridge to an island, you get your first close-up view of one of the tallest hotels in the world at 1,053 feet (321 meters).

3   The chauffeur tells you that the island was built just for the hotel. Construction for the island and the hotel began in 1994 and was finished in 1999 at a cost of $650 million. Nearly 3,500 architects, engineers, and construction staff worked together on this project. The architects designed the hotel to look like the sail of a classical

Arabian ship. This distinctive shape makes people think of adventure, excitement, and luxury. Now it's the symbol of Dubai.

The design team of engineers and architects faced many challenges. To create a strong foundation, they put 250 concrete piles[1] 131 feet deep (40 meters) into the sand and under the sea. To keep the structure safe from high winds and earthquakes, they used over 9,000 tons of steel[2] to support the building. The V-shaped exterior decreases the wind force on the structure. To shape the sail facade, the builders used a material made out of glass. They added a special nonstick layer to the glass. This layer keeps dirt from sticking to the surface of the facade. It is the first time this type of technology was used for such a large surface. **4**

As you enter the hotel, your eyes look up and you admire the tallest atrium[3] in the world. It rises 590 feet (180 meters). A high-speed elevator takes you to your suite on the 14th floor. All 202 suites in this 28-floor hotel have two levels, so there are really 56 floors. Surrounded by gold and marble,[4] you feel like a king or a queen. A personal concierge will be available to you 24 hours a day. He will open doors for you, remember your likes and dislikes, and get you anything you need. You can also expect the latest in technology in your suite. You'll find a laptop computer and at least 10 telephones! However, these luxury amenities are not cheap. A standard suite starts at about $1,500 a night. For $28,000, you can spend the night in the Royal Suite, complete with a private elevator and cinema! **5**

After you check in, take time to decide where to have dinner. There are eight restaurants to choose from. Make sure you visit the Al Muntaha, a restaurant located just below the top floor. It looks like it's floating in the air! At sunset the view is especially beautiful. On another day, consider eating in the Al Mahara, the underwater restaurant. **6**

The Burj Al Arab is an extraordinary engineering achievement. Just visiting this hotel would be the highlight of a trip to Dubai. Staying there would be a dream come true! **7**

---

[1] *piles:* wooden, metal, or concrete columns that are pushed into the ground to support a building
[2] *steel:* a strong metal
[3] *atrium:* a large open space in a building
[4] *marble:* a type of hard stone

4 READING CHECK

A Are these statements true or false? Write *T* (true) or *F* (false).

1 _____ The Burj Al Arab was built on a man-made island.

2 _____ The Burj Al Arab is expensive, but the service is very bad.

3 _____ The Burj Al Arab is an important symbol of the city of Dubai.

B Circle the letter of the best answer.

1 How tall is the Burj Al Arab?
   a 250 feet   **b** 321 feet   **c** 1,053 feet

2 How much did it cost to build the Burj Al Arab?
   a $35,000
   b $202 million
   c $650 million

3 Where is the Burj Al Arab?
   a in Saudi Arabia   **b** in Malaysia   **c** in the United Arab Emirates

4 What is *not* something the Burj Al Arab has?
   a an Arabian ship
   b the world's tallest atrium
   c a high-speed elevator

5 What is the main reason the outside of the building is in a V-shape?
   a It helps keep the surface clean and free from dirt.
   b It makes the hotel look beautiful.
   c It helps protect the structure of the hotel from wind.

6 How many restaurants are there at the Burj Al Arab?
   a 2   **b** 8   **c** 10

7 Which of the following is *not* a job of the concierge?
   a picking up guests at the airport
   b getting a guest something to eat in the middle of the night
   c remembering what a guest likes and doesn't like

8 How much does it cost to stay one night in the Royal Suite?
   a $650
   b $1,500
   c $28,000

5 VOCABULARY CHECK

A Retell the story. Fill in the blanks with the correct words from the box.

amenities	challenge	chauffeur	concierge
concrete	designed	facade	foundation
layer	limousine	project	support

The Burj Al Arab is one of the most luxurious and architecturally unique hotels in the world. The service and _____ are exceptional.

1
A/an _____ picks you up at the airport, and you ride

2
to the hotel in a/an _____ . You meet your personal

3
_____ when you arrive at the hotel. In each suite, you will

4
find the latest in technology.

Building this hotel was a/an _____ . It took five years

5
to complete this _____ . The engineers and architects

6
used _____ piles to make the _____

7   8
strong. The sail _____ was made out of glass and a special

9
nonstick _____ . The engineers _____

10   11
the building to include 9,000 tons of steel, which helps to
_____ it.

12

B In each group, circle the word that does not fit.

1   architect   design   concierge   construct   building

2   facade   window   foundation   structure   challenge

3   chauffeur   greet   limousine   exterior   drive

4   concierge   layer   amenities   suite   service

5   project   design   greet   construct   facade

6 APPLYING READING SKILLS

Your reading speed is the number of words you can read per minute.
Increasing your reading speed *will make it easier to do all the reading for your classes. Timing yourself when you read will help you read faster.*

A Reread "Sail High in the Sky" on page 18, and time yourself. Write your starting time, your finishing time, and the number of minutes it took you to read. Then calculate your reading speed.

> **Story title:** "Sail High in the Sky" (622 words)
>   Starting time: _____
>   Finishing time: _____
>   Total reading time: _____ minutes
> *Reading speed: _____ words per minute

*To calculate your reading speed, divide the number of words in the text (622) by your total reading time (the number of minutes you needed to read the text).

B Now reread either "Ice Hotel" (599 words) on page 4 or "The Traveling Chef" (627 words) on page 11. Time yourself. Write the title of the story and your times below. Then calculate your reading speed.

> **Story title:** _____ (_____ words)
> Starting time: _____
> Finishing time: _____
> Total reading time: _____ minutes
> Reading speed: _____ words per minute

7 DISCUSSION

Discuss the following questions in pairs or groups.

1 If you had the money, would you stay in the Burj Al Arab? Explain.
2 What do you think is the most interesting feature of the Burj Al Arab? Explain.
3 If you could design a luxury hotel, how would you design it?

VOCABULARY REVIEW

Chapter 1	Chapter 2	Chapter 3
Tourism and Hospitality	**Tourism and Hospitality**	**Tourism and Hospitality**
book (v.) · **check in** (v.) · **destination** · (take an) **excursion** · **pack** (v.) · (luxury) **suite**	**guide** (n.) · **museum** · **scenery** · **souvenir**	**amenities** · **chauffeur** · **concierge** · **greet** · **limousine**
Academic Word List	**Academic Word List**	**Academic Word List**
appreciate · **approach** (v.) · **construct** · **predict** · **unique**	**distinct** · **diverse** · **interaction** · **reluctant** · **significant** · **traditional**	**challenge** (n.) · **design** (v.) · **foundation** · **layer** (n.) · **project** (n.) · **structure** (n.)
Art	**Culinary Arts**	**Engineering**
architect · **carve** · **gallery** · **sculpture**	**beverage** · **cuisine** · **fried** · **recipe** · **spice**	**concrete** (n.) · **exterior** · **facade** · **support** (v.)

Find words in the chart that match the definitions. Answers to 1–4 are from Chapter 1.
Answers to 5–8 are from Chapter 2. Answers to 9–12 are from Chapter 3.

1 To make something by cutting into a hard material: _____

2 To report your arrival at a hotel: _____

3 To come nearer to something or someone: _____

4 A short trip usually for pleasure, often by a group of people: _____

5 Different or varied: _____

6 Instructions for preparing and cooking a particular food: _____

7 A flavoring for food: _____

8 Something you keep to remind you of a special place: _____

9 Something that was built, such as a building or a bridge: _____

10 A large, luxurious car, usually with a driver: _____

11 The front of a building: _____

12 To make or draw plans for something: _____

VOCABULARY IN USE

Work with a partner or small group, and discuss the questions below.

1 What is **distinct** about your hometown? Explain.

2 What is the biggest **challenge** right now for the leader of your country?

3 What was a **significant** event in your life in the last five years? Explain.

4 Where do you think is the best **destination** for a honeymoon? Explain.

5 If you were a **chauffeur**, what famous person would you like to drive around?

6 What is one thing that you are **reluctant** to do? Explain.

7 What is your favorite **beverage**? Explain.

8 What new technology do you **predict** will be popular in five years?

ROLE PLAY

Work with a partner. One student is a travel agent. The other student is a client. Role-play a meeting in which the travel agent asks questions and the client answers.

Travel agent: Prepare general questions to ask the client about preferences for dates of travel, destinations, types of hotels and restaurants, and things to do.

Client: Prepare a list of preferences for dates of travel, destinations, types of hotels and restaurants you like, and things you would like to do.

WRITING

Imagine you are one of these people: Karen or Paul Anderson, Andrew Zimmern, or a guest at the Burj Al Arab. Write an e-mail message to a friend, and include the following information.

- Explain where you are and what you did today.

- Describe any interesting people you have met.

- Describe the most significant thing you have experienced so far.

WEBQUEST

Find more information about the topics in this unit by going on the Internet. Go to www.cambridge.org/readthis and follow the instructions for doing a WebQuest. Search for facts. Have fun. Good luck!

Chapter 4

The Mysterious Disappearance of *Kaiko*

A research ship goes down to the deepest place on Earth and then suddenly disappears.

Content areas:
- Earth Science
- Engineering

Chapter 5

An Ocean of Plastic

On a sailing trip through unknown waters, a sailor discovers a shocking environmental problem.

Content areas:
- Earth Science
- Environmental Studies

Chapter 6

Ed Pulaski and the Big Burn

One firefighter's brave actions save a group of men trapped by a terrible fire.

Content areas:
- Earth Science
- Forestry

The Mysterious Disappearance of *Kaiko*

1 TOPIC PREVIEW

A Which things do you think you would find at the deepest place in the ocean? Put a check (✓) next to the things you might find. Share your answers with your classmates.

1 _____ very large fish

2 _____ plants

3 _____ cold temperatures

4 _____ hot temperatures

5 _____ _____ (your idea)

B Read the title of this chapter, look at the picture, and discuss the following questions.

1 What activities can you do in the ocean? Have you ever gone surfing or scuba diving?

2 Do you think the ocean can be dangerous? Explain.

3 What do you think the reading is going to be about?

2 VOCABULARY PREVIEW

A Read the word lists. Put a check (✓) next to the words that you know and can use in a sentence. Compare your answers with a partner. Then look up any unfamiliar words in a dictionary.

Earth Science	Academic Word List	Engineering
elevation explore ocean floor (above / below) **sea level** surface (*n.*) trench	complex (make) **contact** monitor (*v.*) release (*v.*) survey (*v.*)	electronic float (*v.*) pressure robot

The chart shows selected words from the reading related to earth science, engineering, and the Academic Word List (AWL). For more information about the AWL, see page 121.

B Fill in the blanks with words from Part A.

1 A big city is a/an _____ place, with many different sections.

2 A piece of wood will _____ on water. A rock will not.

3 The mountain known as K2 has a/an _____ of 28,251 feet (8,611 meters).

4 After the storm, I could not make _____ with anyone by phone.

5 He stood on top of the hill so he could _____ the valley below.

6 In that factory, a/an _____ now does work that people once did.

7 The store sells _____ items like TVs, computers, and phones.

8 The island is only a few feet above _____ , so it floods easily.

9 The _____ of the lake was very smooth, without any waves.

10 The farmers dug a/an _____ to carry rainwater to their fields.

11 No one has been able to _____ some parts of Antarctica.

12 If you put a lot of _____ on glass, it will break.

13 The *Titanic* sank long ago. Now it lies on the _____ .

14 The boy opened the door of the cage to _____ the bird inside.

15 Parents and teachers will _____ the students during the trip.

Preview the questions in Reading Check Part A on page 30. Then read the story.

The Mysterious Disappearance of *Kaiko*

Kaiko

1   For eight years, a tough little submarine[1] worked in the deepest, darkest place on Earth. It explored the ocean floor in terrible conditions. The pressure there is about 1,000 times greater than at the ocean's surface. No light from the sun ever reaches so deep. Then the submarine, *Kaiko*, suddenly disappeared. What happened? Did the extreme conditions kill *Kaiko*? Where did *Kaiko* go?

2   Researchers in Japan wanted *Kaiko* to explore the bottom of the Mariana Trench and look for living things deep in the sea. In fact, the name *Kaiko* means "trench" in Japanese. The Mariana Trench is a deep opening in the floor of the Pacific Ocean, near the island of Guam. The bottom of the trench is nearly 7 miles (11.27 kilometers) below sea level. Compare this depth to the height of Mount Everest, Earth's highest mountain. Everest's elevation is only about 5.5 miles (8.85 kilometers) above sea level.

3   In 1960, Jacques Piccard of Switzerland and Donald Walsh of the United States traveled to the trench bottom in a submarine named *Trieste*. It went down more than 35,790 feet (10,909 meters) below the surface to the ocean floor. Piccard and Walsh were in constant danger.

---

[1] *submarine:* a ship that travels under water

The deep water put terrible stress on *Trieste*. The ship's windows started to crack, so Piccard and Walsh had to come to the surface as quickly as possible. They had no time to survey the bottom at these great depths.

Kaiko could stay down longer than *Trieste* because *Kaiko* was a robot. No human was inside. The scientists who controlled it floated safely in a research ship on the ocean surface. They monitored the dive through electronic equipment such as television cameras. *Kaiko*'s trip to the ocean floor was like a Moon landing. A larger "mother ship" went most of the way to the bottom and then released *Kaiko*. The mother ship stayed nearby, ready to take *Kaiko* back after its exploration was finished.

4

Kaiko's first successful trip to the bottom of the trench was on March 24, 1995. After it made contact with the ocean floor, it planted a simple plaque:[2] "*Kaiko* 1995.3.24." The robot took a few samples of bottom sand. Then it rose slightly to take some water samples. After about two hours, *Kaiko* went back to the mother ship and then went home.

5

Kaiko brought back amazing information. More than 180 living things were in its sample containers. As scientists had expected, the animals and plants *Kaiko* collected were extremely small. The submarine's cameras, however, told a surprising story. They sent back pictures of much larger living things like a shrimp, a worm, and a sea cucumber. Scientists had never expected to find such complex life so deep in the ocean.

6

Over the next eight years, *Kaiko* continued to explore deep parts of the Pacific Ocean. Then, in 2003, a terrible thing happened. A dangerous storm was approaching. The scientists who controlled *Kaiko* hurried to pull the submarine back up to the surface, but they were shocked to find only an empty cable.[3] *Kaiko* was not there.

7

Kaiko's disappearance is still a mystery. What broke its cable? Where is it? As late as 2006, a few radio signals from *Kaiko* reached researchers. This meant it was probably on or near the surface, not on the ocean floor. The Pacific, however, is the world's biggest ocean. In an area so large, the tough little explorer may never be found.

8

---

[2] *plaque:* a sign meant to last a long time, usually made of metal or some other hard material

[3] *cable:* a rope made of metal

4 READING CHECK

A Are these statements true or false? Write *T* (true) or *F* (false).

1 ____ Scientists used *Kaiko* to explore the ocean floor.

2 ____ *Kaiko* was the first ship to go to the bottom of the Mariana Trench.

3 ____ No animals or plants can live in the deepest place on Earth.

B Circle the letter of the best answer.

1 Where were the scientists who controlled *Kaiko* from?
   a Japan   **b** Guam   **c** the United States

2 How does the depth of the Mariana Trench compare to the height of Mount Everest?
   a Its depth is about the same as the height of Mount Everest.
   b Its depth is greater than the height of Mount Everest.
   c Its depth is less than the height of Mount Everest.

3 Why did the men inside *Trieste* quickly leave the bottom of the trench?
   a They could not breathe.
   b They could not see anything.
   c Their ship started to break.

4 What did *Kaiko*'s "mother ship" do?
   a It carried *Kaiko* most of the way to the ocean floor.
   b It carried the researchers who controlled *Kaiko*.
   c It carried the equipment that monitored *Kaiko*.

5 When did *Kaiko* first reach the bottom of the Mariana Trench?
   a in 1960   **b** in 1995   **c** in 2003

6 How did *Kaiko* get 180 living things to bring back to the researchers?
   a It planted a plaque.   **b** It took samples.   **c** It took pictures.

7 Why did scientists hurry to bring *Kaiko* back in 2003?
   a Its cable was breaking.
   b A storm was coming.
   c Radio signals were coming from it.

8 Where is *Kaiko* today?
   a floating in the Pacific
   b on the ocean floor
   c No one knows.

5 VOCABULARY CHECK

A Retell the story. Fill in the blanks with the correct words from the box.

complex	electronic	elevation	explore	monitored
ocean floor	pressure	robot	sea level	trench

The deepest place on Earth is a/an _____ on

the _____ of the Pacific. It is about 7 miles below

2

_____ . This depth is much greater than the

3

_____ of Earth's highest mountain. Two men went

4

down there in 1960, but they had to leave quickly because extreme

_____ started to crush their ship.

5

In the 1990s, *Kaiko* was built to _____ this area

6

more safely. *Kaiko* was a/an _____ with no one inside.

7

Scientists _____ *Kaiko* and controlled its movements by

8

using _____ equipment. *Kaiko* reached this deep part

9

of the Pacific in 1995. It found both simple and _____

10

forms of life there. *Kaiko* returned to this area many more times before it

disappeared in 2003.

B Write a short paragraph about *Kaiko*. Use the following words: *contact, float, surface, survey,* and *release*. Use the correct verb tense or the correct singular or plural noun form.

_____

_____

_____

_____

_____

_____

_____

_____

6 APPLYING READING SKILLS

> *A pronoun (he, them, that, etc.) refers to (has the same meaning as) a noun or noun phrase that comes before or after it.* **Finding the correct pronoun reference** *in a reading is an important skill.*

A Which noun or noun phrase does the underlined pronoun refer to? Circle the noun or noun phrase and draw an arrow from the underlined word to it.

1 The bottom is more than 7 miles underwater. No sunlight reaches <u>it</u>.

2 Walsh and Piccard quickly left the trench because <u>they</u> were in danger.

3 In <u>its</u> sample containers, *Kaiko* had more than 180 living things.

4 *Kaiko* collected plants and animals. As scientists expected, <u>they</u> were very small.

5 The Pacific is huge. Scientists know <u>they</u> may never find *Kaiko*.

B Go back to the reading, and find the answers to the following questions.

SENTENCE FROM THE READING	QUESTION	ANSWER
It went down more than 35,790 feet (10,909 meters) below the surface to the ocean floor.	What does *it* refer to?	
They sent back pictures of much larger living things like a shrimp, a worm, and a sea cucumber.	What does *they* refer to?	
This meant it was probably on or near the surface, not on the ocean floor.	What does *this* refer to? What does *it* refer to?	

7 DISCUSSION

Discuss the following questions in pairs or groups.

1 Where is *Kaiko*? Do you think it will ever be found?

2 Would you rather go to the top of Mount Everest or to the bottom of the Mariana Trench? Explain.

3 It is expensive to explore the ocean floor. Do you think it is a good use of money? What do you think scientists are looking for and may find?

CHAPTER
5
An Ocean of Plastic

1 TOPIC PREVIEW

A How many items that you often use are plastic? Put a check (✓) next to each one. Share your answers with your classmates.

1 _____ a toothbrush

2 _____ food containers (boxes, bags, etc.)

3 _____ water bottles

4 _____ things to wear (clothes, jewelry, etc.)

5 _____ _____ (your idea)

B Read the title of this chapter, look at the picture, and discuss the following questions.

1 What do cities and towns do with plastic garbage? Explain.

2 Describe this picture. What do you think is happening? Where do you think you might see something like this? Have you ever seen anything like this? Explain.

3 What do you think the reading is going to be about?

2 VOCABULARY PREVIEW

A Read the word lists. Put a check (✓) next to the words that you know and can use in a sentence. Compare your answers with a partner. Then look up any unfamiliar words in a dictionary.

Earth Science	Academic Word List	Environmental Studies
(ocean) **current** **flow** (*v.*) **oceanographer** **satellite**	**chemical** (*n.*) **disposable** **expert** (*n.*) **process** (*n.*) **region** **reveal**	**bacteria** **break down** (*v.*) **organic** **spill** (*v.*) **toxin**

The chart shows selected words from the reading related to earth science, environmental studies, and the Academic Word List (AWL). For more information about the AWL, see page 121.

B Fill in the blanks with words from Part A.

1 A/an _____ from a factory next to the lake killed the fish.

2 A/an _____ in the ocean carried the ship to Mexico.

3 The _____ circles Earth and monitors the planet's weather.

4 Many _____ can live only in water and die if they dry out.

5 The _____ of getting a driver's license involves three steps.

6 He is a/an _____ on the plays of William Shakespeare.

7 Putting _____ material into your garden makes the soil richer.

8 A/an _____ discovered that the sea was getting warmer.

9 Most people forget that water is a/an _____ , known as H_2O.

10 The TV reviewer did not _____ how the movie ended.

11 Some rivers in the Americas _____ into the Pacific Ocean.

12 Be careful when you pour the milk so you don't _____ it.

13 Plastic does not _____ very quickly, so it collects in the ocean.

14 One _____ of the country gets a lot of rain, but others are dry.

15 They brought _____ plates and cups to the picnic.

Preview the questions in Reading Check Part A on page 37. Then read the story.

An Ocean of Plastic

A big part of the Pacific Ocean is choking[1] on a huge sea of plastic garbage. Some scientists think it's as large as the United States, but almost no one noticed it until 1997. Then, an adventurer named Charles Moore made a shocking discovery, and scientists learned the ugly truth.

Moore was the captain of a sailboat that had just completed a race. He planned to sail home from Hawaii to California. The usual route went south, then east. The winds are strong there, and boats move quickly. Moore, however, was not in a hurry. He decided to sail directly east – a slow route with weak winds. This region gets few visitors, so Moore was sailing into almost unknown waters.

What Moore found in the lonely North Pacific was a shock. Floating under the ocean's surface was a "soup" of plastic garbage. It was thick with billions of tiny plastic pieces the size of apple seeds. They made a clicking sound against the sides of the boat as it sailed along. Everyday plastic objects, such as shopping bags and water bottles, were trapped among the tiny pieces. In the middle of the ocean, a thousand miles from the nearest town, the sea of garbage stretched as far as Moore could see.

Moore and Curtis Ebbesmeyer, a researcher, began calling this area the Great Garbage Patch.[2] Ebbesmeyer was an expert in ocean

---

[1] *choking:* unable to breathe or survive because something blocks the movement of air

[2] *patch:* an area that is different in some way from the area that surrounds it

garbage. In the 1990s, he studied shipping accidents that spilled big loads of sports shoes and plastic bath toys into the ocean. Ocean currents pushed the shoes and toys along. The movement of the objects revealed where currents flow in some parts of the Pacific.

5   Oceanographers are not surprised that garbage collects in the North Pacific. A pattern of winds and currents, called the North Pacific Gyre, gathers this garbage. Water in the gyre goes round and round in a clockwise[3] pattern, and anything that gets into the middle of it is trapped. This natural process has continued for millions of years. Organic garbage, such as food, tree branches, and paper, gets broken down by bacteria and chemicals. It returns to its original parts and re-enters the environment. The difference is that now most of the garbage is plastic, and plastic is inorganic. Bacteria and chemicals in the seawater cannot break it down. Plastic will therefore stay in the environment for hundreds or even thousands of years.

6   Some oceanographers doubted Moore's reports. Why didn't satellite pictures show the patch? Where did all this plastic come from? Is it really a problem? If so, how do we solve it? Moore learned some answers during return trips to the Great Garbage Patch. Satellites don't see the plastic because most of it hides under the ocean's surface. Some of the plastic comes from ships, but most of it is washed into the ocean from cities beside the Pacific.

7   The Great Garbage Patch is a real problem because the plastic in it is harmful to animals. To fish and birds, a piece of plastic can look like food. The animal eats it, and the plastic gets stuck inside. This makes it harder for an animal to eat real food. Toxins from ocean water also get into the body of an animal because toxins stick to the plastic. These poisonous chemicals can kill the animal or make it sick.

8   Moore cannot answer the biggest question: What can we do about it? The patch is too big and too deep to clean up. Even if someone could remove all today's plastic from the ocean, new garbage would soon take its place. People will not stop using plastic. In fact, many plastic items, such as knives and forks, are designed to be disposable. As cities near the Pacific grow bigger, the amount washing into the ocean grows too. For now, Moore can only gather facts about the Great Garbage Patch and make sure the world pays attention to this serious environmental problem.

---

[3] *clockwise:* moving in the same direction as the hands on a clock

4 READING CHECK

A Are these statements true or false? Write *T* (true) or *F* (false).

1 _____ In 1997, Moore found a garbage patch in the ocean by accident.

2 _____ In the past, the North Pacific Gyre had non-plastic garbage.

3 _____ Moore is now trying to remove the plastic from the garbage patch.

B Circle the letter of the best answer.

1 What was Moore doing when he discovered the garbage patch?
   a conducting research   **b** sailing in a race   **c** sailing home

2 Why was the garbage patch not well known before Moore found it?
   a Few people sail through that part of the Pacific.
   b Earlier scientists wanted to keep it a secret.
   c People sailing through it cannot see the plastic.

3 How did Ebbesmeyer study ocean currents in the 1990s?
   a by sailing through the garbage patch
   b by watching the movements of plastic garbage
   c by examining satellite pictures of the North Pacific

4 What makes the water in a gyre go around in a clockwise direction?
   a bacteria and chemicals
   b plastic and other garbage
   c wind and currents

5 How is the Great Garbage Patch different now from earlier times?
   a Most of the garbage there is inorganic.
   b Fish and birds now live there.
   c It is now in the middle of a gyre.

6 Where does most of the plastic in the patch come from?
   a ships   **b** cities   **c** animals

7 Why is the Great Garbage Patch a big problem?
   a The plastic in it can harm animals.
   b Boats cannot move through it.
   c It contains no real food for animals.

8 What is Moore trying to do about the garbage patch?
   a clean up the plastic in it
   b get people to use less plastic
   c make people more aware of it

5 VOCABULARY CHECK

A Retell the story. Fill in the blanks with the correct words from the box.

bacteria	chemicals	currents	disposable	expert
oceanographers	organic	region	satellite	toxins

In 1997, a sailor named Charles Moore discovered that part of the Pacific Ocean is filled with plastic garbage. Some _____
questioned Moore's findings. They asked why this big area could not be seen in _____ photos. But others agreed with Moore. He and Curtis Ebbesmeyer, a/an _____ on ocean garbage, named this _____ of the Pacific "the Great Garbage Patch." There, ocean _____ and winds push the water around in a clockwise circle. Garbage collects when it gets trapped inside.

Once, most of the garbage in the patch was _____ , made of natural materials. _____ would break it down, so it re-entered the environment. Now most of the garbage is plastic that comes from _____ items like bottles or bags. Animals sometimes try to eat the plastic, which often has _____ stuck to it. These poisonous _____ may build up in the animals and kill them. So far, no one has found a way to clean up the Great Garbage Patch.

B Circle the word that does not fit. Use a dictionary if necessary.

1 Things that people **reveal**:   information   a secret   a storm

2 Things that have a **process**:   sea animals   education   cooking

3 Things that **flow**:   a river   a ship   air

4 Things that people **spill**:   milk   buildings   salt

5 Things that **break down**:   paper   leaves   plastic

6 APPLYING READING SKILLS

You will often read about how one event causes another event to happen. ***Finding causes and effects*** *in a reading can help you understand the reading better.*

A Match the cause on the left with its effect on the right.

1 ____ Bacteria and chemicals break the garbage down.	**a**	The garbage patch was almost unknown until 1997.
2 ____ Plastic gathers poisonous chemicals in the seawater.	**b**	Garbage collects in one area of the Pacific.
3 ____ Few people sail near the location of the garbage patch.	**c**	Organic material re-enters the natural environment.
4 ____ A pattern of ocean currents keeps objects from escaping.	**d**	Toxins build up inside the bodies of sea animals.

B Find one effect in the text for each cause.

CAUSE	EFFECT
1 Charles Moore sailed home by an unusual route.	
2 Curtis Ebbesmeyer studied how objects floated in the ocean after shipping accidents.	
3 The plastic in the garbage patch floats under the surface of the ocean, not on top.	
4 Bacteria and chemicals in seawater cannot break plastic down.	

7 DISCUSSION

Discuss the following questions in pairs or groups.

1 Is Moore right to claim that the garbage patch is a problem even though it's far away from cities and people?

2 Can you think of any ways to remove the plastic from the Pacific? Explain.

3 What are some reasons for using less plastic? What are some ways we can do this?

Ed Pulaski and the Big Burn

1 TOPIC PREVIEW

A Imagine that you are in a forest and a fire starts coming toward you. What would you do? Put a check (✓) next to the things you might do. Share your answers with your classmates.

1 _____ run away

2 _____ stay and fight the fire

3 _____ jump into a river or a lake

4 _____ dig a hole and hide

5 _____ _____ (your idea)

B Read the title of this chapter, look at the picture, and discuss the following questions.

1 What does the picture show? Explain.

2 What are the causes of fires in nature? Do fires like this happen near where you live?

3 What do you think the reading is going to be about?

2 VOCABULARY PREVIEW

A Read the word lists. Put a check (✓) next to the words that you know and can use in a sentence. Compare your answers with a partner. Then look up any unfamiliar words in a dictionary.

Earth Science	Academic Word List	Forestry
lightning thunderstorm tornado vegetation wildfire	cycle (*n.*) establish intense survive	ash blaze (*n.*) chop (*v.*) flame seed set fire to

The chart shows selected words from the reading related to earth science, forestry, and the Academic Word List (AWL). For more information about the AWL, see page 121.

B Write the word from Part A next to its definition.

1 An uncontrolled fire in a field or a forest: _____

2 A bright flash of light in the sky during a storm: _____

3 To hit something with a sharp tool in order to cut it: _____

4 A dark gray powder left after something has burned: _____

5 One small part of a fire: _____

6 Plants: _____

7 A process that starts again after reaching its end: _____

8 To start something that becomes permanent later: _____

9 A small object that a plant can grow from: _____

10 To make something begin to burn: _____

11 To stay alive despite an event that could have killed you: _____

12 Weather with bright flashes of light and loud sounds: _____

13 A big fire: _____

14 Very strong: _____

15 Violent weather with very strong, circular winds: _____

Preview the questions in Reading Check Part A on page 44. Then read the story.

Ed Pulaski and the Big Burn

1   It was August 1910, in the American West. The worst wildfire in
U.S. history, called the Big Burn, was roaring toward Ed Pulaski
and his crew[1] of firefighters. The intense heat cooked fish alive in the
rivers, and rocks exploded around them. Surrounded by flames and
with nowhere to run, many of Pulaski's men thought they would soon
be dead.

2   The firefighters were trying to stop one of nature's most powerful
forces. Forests in the American West go through natural cycles of fire
and re-growth. A wildfire burns away old trees, clearing space for new
ones. Certain types of trees cannot reproduce without fire. Their seeds
are released only when intense heat melts the covering around them.

3   Many wildfires start during dry thunderstorms that occur in the
mountains in the summertime. These storms bring almost no rain,
but they produce lightning that sets fire to dry grasses and dead wood.
The American Indians knew how to live with these fires. Sometimes
they even set their own fires to clear paths through the forests. By the
early 1900s, new settlers had moved west and had established towns
and farms. To them, fire was an enemy.

4   Ed Pulaski lived in one of these towns, Wallace, Idaho, which was
in the path of the Big Burn. While his wife stayed in town with their
baby, Pulaski and his men marched toward the fire. Their plan was to

---

[1] *crew:* a group of people who get together to complete a task

remove the trees, bushes, and grass at the fire's edge. Without this dry vegetation, they thought the flames would probably die out.

However, the Big Burn was too big to fight. Dozens of smaller fires 5
had combined into one big, terrible blaze, which got even worse when strong winds blew in from the northwest. The fire was lifted into the tops of the trees. Burning wood flew 10 miles (16 kilometers) away and started new fires. Flames 300 feet (91.5 meters) high rose over the frightened firefighters. A fire that big is a monster. It makes its own weather, sucking air into its center and twisting like a tornado. Pulaski forgot about firefighting and focused on saving the lives of the 45 men who were with him.

Even though Pulaski could hardly see, he managed to find an 6
opening in the earth. It was the entrance to an old mine.[2] He ordered his men to go into the mine. Some resisted because the air inside was filled with smoke and was as hot as an oven. It would be a terrible place to die. Some men tried to run out, but Pulaski grabbed his gun and threatened to shoot anyone who ran away.

Flaming sticks were flying into the mine. The wood that supported 7
the roof of the mine was catching fire. Pulaski went to the mine entrance and fought the flames with horse blankets. He found water dripping through the roof of the mine, collected it in his hat, and threw it on the flames.

The hot, smoky air inside the mine became so hard for the men 8
to breathe that they fell to the ground, unconscious. Finally, the fire roared past, and most of the men had survived. After the survivors woke up, they made their way toward the light at the mine entrance. There they discovered Pulaski on the ground, his unmoving body covered with ashes. One of the men said that the boss was dead, but then a voice from the ashes told the man he was wrong. Ed Pulaski was very much alive.

The town of Wallace was partly destroyed in the fire, but Pulaski's 9
family survived. Ed Pulaski continued fighting wildfires, and he found many new, better ways for firefighters to do their job. Even now, more than a century later, firefighters remember him daily as they face forest fires. Their main hand tool, which combines a chopping end with a digging end, is called a *pulaski*.

---

[2] *mine:* a deep hole in the ground where people (called *miners*) dig out coal or other natural material

4 READING CHECK

A Are these statements true or false? Write *T* (true) or *F* (false).

1 _____ Ed Pulaski believed wildfires are good and should not be fought.

2 _____ Firefighters can control fires by removing plants that can burn.

3 _____ An underground mine protected Pulaski's men from the flames.

B Circle the letter of the best answer.

1 Why was the Big Burn unusual?
   a It occurred in the American West.
   b People tried to fight it.
   c It was an extremely bad wildfire.

2 How do wildfires fit into natural processes?
   a They make room for new trees to grow.
   b They prevent people from settling in natural areas.
   c They help cause dry thunderstorms.

3 How did new settlers differ from American Indians?
   a They learned to live with wildfires.
   b They lived in the West.
   c They fought wildfires.

4 What was true about Wallace, Idaho?
   a Pulaski's crew removed vegetation from it.
   b It was far away from the Big Burn.
   c Pulaski's family lived there.

5 What made the Big Burn even worse?
   a strong winds
   b tornadoes
   c firefighters

6 Why did Pulaski grab his gun?
   a to fight the fire at the mine entrance
   b to keep his men from leaving the mine
   c to protect his men from others in the mine

7 What contribution by Pulaski is still used today?
   a the use of mines during fires
   b a method for saving towns
   c a tool for firefighting

5 VOCABULARY CHECK

A Retell the story. Fill in the blanks with the correct words from the box.

blaze	cycles	established	flames	intense
lightning	survived	thunderstorms	vegetation	wildfires

In the American West, _____ are part of
nature. A typical forest stays healthy by going through regular
_____ of fire and re-growth. Many of these fires occur
after the _____ from _____ strikes dry
_____ . As more people moved to the West in the 1900s,
they _____ towns and farms.

In 1910, some firefighters led by Ed Pulaski went out to fight a large and
terrible _____ near Wallace, Idaho. They couldn't fight it,
however, because the fire was too _____ . It was the Big
Burn, the largest such fire in U.S. history. Rising hundreds of feet into the
air, _____ from the fire trapped Pulaski and his men. To
save them, Pulaski made them go underground in an old mine. Thanks to
Pulaski's leadership, almost all the men _____ .

B Certain words often go together. These are called *collocations*. Fill in the blanks
with words from the box to form some common collocations with the words
in bold.

covered	planted	set	struck	trees

1 A really strong **tornado** _____ the town.

2 The firefighters used axes to **chop** _____ **down**.

3 Sometimes American Indians _____ **fire to** trees in
   order to clear paths in the forest.

4 The farmer _____ **seeds** in the fields.

5 Ed Pulaski was _____ **with** ashes, and he was
   not moving.

6 APPLYING READING SKILLS

Understanding the order of events in a reading means that you know what happens first, second, third, and so on. Making a time line is an excellent way to help you keep track of the order of events.

A Write the letter of the following events into the time line in the correct order.

a Ed Pulaski and his family settled in Wallace, Idaho.

b Fires were a natural process in the American West.

c Firefighters use a hand tool called a *pulaski*.

d Pulaski told his men he was not dead.

e Flames from the Big Burn surrounded Pulaski and his men.

f Pulaski led his men into an old mine.

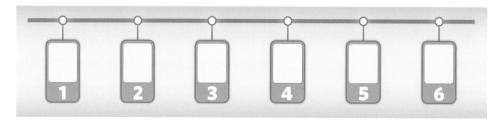

B Circle the correct word for each sentence. Use information from your time line in Part A and the reading.

1 American Indians settled in the American West (before / after) the 1900s.

2 Pulaski grabbed his gun (before / after) he led his men into the mine.

3 Pulaski and his wife had a child (before / after) the Big Burn.

4 Certain trees reproduce only (before / after) a fire affects their seeds.

7 DISCUSSION

Discuss the following questions in pairs or groups.

1 Have you ever been near a big fire? Were you in danger? How was it fought?

2 How do you think firefighting equipment is different today from 1910? Explain.

3 Ed Pulaski showed great bravery. Can you think of other examples of brave behavior that have been in the news recently?

VOCABULARY REVIEW

Chapter 4	Chapter 5	Chapter 6
Earth Science	**Earth Science**	**Earth Science**
elevation · explore · ocean floor · (above / below) sea level · surface (*n.*) · trench	(ocean) current · flow (*v.*) · oceanographer · satellite	lightning · thunderstorm · tornado · vegetation · wildfire
Academic Word List	**Academic Word List**	**Academic Word List**
complex · (make) contact · monitor (*v.*) · release (*v.*) · survey (*v.*)	chemical (*n.*) · disposable · expert (*n.*) · process (*n.*) · region · reveal	cycle (*n.*) · establish · intense · survive
Engineering	**Environmental Studies**	**Forestry**
electronic · float (*v.*) · pressure · robot	bacteria · break down (*v.*) · organic · spill (*v.*) · toxin	ash · blaze (*n.*) · chop (*v.*) · lame · seed · set fire to

Find words in the chart that match the definitions. Answers to 1–4 are from Chapter 4. Answers to 5–8 are from Chapter 5. Answers to 9–12 are from Chapter 6.

1 To stay on top of a liquid instead of sinking: _____

2 To look at an area of land: _____

3 The top or outside of something: _____

4 Not simple: _____

5 A piece of equipment sent into space to circle Earth: _____

6 Very small living things that sometimes cause disease: _____

7 A large area or part: _____

8 Someone who studies the sea: _____

9 A small object that a plant can grow from: _____

10 A dark gray powder left after something has burned: _____

11 A bright flash of light in the sky during a storm: _____

12 A process that starts again after reaching its end: _____

VOCABULARY IN USE

Work with a partner or small group, and discuss the questions below.

1 How many **electronic** things do you own? What are they?

2 Are there any places on Earth left to **explore**? Where are they?

3 If you could be an **expert** in one subject, what would you choose? Explain.

4 How closely should parents **monitor** Internet use by their children? Explain.

5 Should you ever **reveal** a secret that a friend told you? Explain.

6 If you were in a building when a fire started, what would you do to **survive**?

7 Name some **disposable** things you use. Do you use too many? Explain.

8 If you are far from a building when a bad **thunderstorm** strikes, what should you do?

ROLE PLAY

Work with a partner. You are going to debate this statement: *Life on Earth will be much worse in 100 years because human beings are destroying the natural environment.* Student A will speak for two minutes, and then Student B will speak for two minutes. When you have both finished, challenge each other's opinions.

Student A: You believe life on Earth will be much worse in 100 years. Prepare a list of your reasons. Be prepared to explain your reasons.

Student B: You believe that life on Earth will not be much worse in 100 years. Prepare a list of your reasons. Be prepared to explain your reasons.

WRITING

Imagine that you are Jacques Piccard, Charles Moore, or Ed Pulaski, and you have your own Web site. Write a blog entry. As you write, answer the following questions.

- What happened to you today?

- What actions did you take in response to what happened?

- What are your opinions about the relationship between humans and nature?

WEBQUEST

Find more information about the topics in this unit by going on the Internet. Go to www.cambridge.org/readthis and follow the instructions for doing a WebQuest. Search for facts. Have fun. Good luck!

UNIT

3

Sports and Fitness

Chapter 7

The Flying Housewife

She has been called the greatest female athlete of the twentieth century. Why?

Content areas:
- Sports and Fitness
- Sociology

Chapter 8

The Big Fish

What's that swimming in the water? Is it a fish? No, it's Martin Strel, an extraordinary long-distance swimmer.

Content areas:
- Sports and Fitness
- Environmental Studies

Chapter 9

Blade Runner

This young South African was a very fast runner, but some people did not want him to run in the Olympics.

Content areas:
- Sports and Fitness
- Biomedical Engineering

7

The Flying Housewife

1 TOPIC PREVIEW

A Match the woman in the left column with the sport she played or plays in the right column. Share your answers with your classmates.

1 _____ Nadia Comaneci	**a**	Golf
2 _____ Maria Sharapova	**b**	Soccer
3 _____ Michelle Kwan	**c**	Tennis
4 _____ Se Ri Pak	**d**	Gymnastics
5 _____ Guo Jingjing	**e**	Ice-skating
6 _____ Mia Hamm	**f**	Diving

B Read the title of this chapter, look at the picture, and discuss the following questions.

1 Who are some famous female sports stars in the country you live in? What sports do they play?

2 Why do you think the woman in the picture is called "The Flying Housewife"? Explain.

3 What do you think the reading is going to be about?

2 VOCABULARY PREVIEW

A Read the word lists. Put a check (✓) next to the words that you know and can use in a sentence. Compare your answers with a partner. Then look up any unfamiliar words in a dictionary.

Sports and Fitness	Academic Word List	Sociology
athlete coach (*n.*) compete set (a) record talented train (*v.*)	conventional individual (*adj.*) participation	career disapprove (of) encourage forbid society unacceptable

The chart shows selected words from the reading related to sports and fitness, sociology, and the Academic Word List (AWL). For more information about the AWL, see page 121.

B Fill in the blanks with words from Part A.

1 The young doctor wanted to have a/an _____ in sports medicine.

2 A good _____ practices his or her sport daily.

3 The baseball _____ had his players practice hitting the ball.

4 The high school swimmer _____ for winning the most races.

5 He is a very _____ man. He always wears a suit and tie.

6 The parents _____ their children to play dangerous sports.

7 _____ in every game was required for all the players.

8 The _____ college sports star became a famous soccer player.

9 Fitness experts _____ people to stretch before they exercise.

10 People often behave according to the traditions of their _____ .

11 Golf is a/an _____ sport; basketball is a team sport.

12 Cheating during a game is _____ !

13 The skier is preparing to _____ in the Olympics next year.

14 People generally _____ of telling lies.

15 To do his or her best, a gymnast must _____ every day.

Preview the questions in Reading Check Part A on page 54. Then read the story.

The Flying Housewife

Fanny Blankers-Koen, 1948

Dara Torres, 2008

1   When forty-one-year-old American swimmer Dara Torres, mother of a two-year-old, competed in the 2008 Beijing Olympics, people were surprised. They did not disapprove. They just thought that it would be difficult for an older athlete and a new mother to compete against younger athletes. Why, then, did people disapprove when runner Fanny Blankers-Koen, a thirty-year-old Dutch mother with two young children, competed in the Olympics? The year was 1948, and things were very different for women at that time.

2   Today, many women compete in sports, but society hasn't always allowed their participation. In ancient Greece, women were forbidden to compete in the Olympic Games. When the modern Olympics began in 1896, women were still not allowed to participate. It was not until the second modern Olympics of 1900 that women were finally allowed to join the all-male competition. Society still thought that women were too weak for many sports. They could only participate in less physically demanding sports, such as archery, golf, and ice-skating. Many female athletes found these rules unacceptable. By the 1930s, therefore, Olympic officials made some changes. They allowed women to compete in *some* track-and-field[1] events, but in no more than three individual events.

---

[1] *track-and-field:* sporting events performed on a running track or on the field near the track

Fanny Blankers-Koen was one of many female athletes in the 1930s. She grew up in an active family and played sports. Her natural athleticism was encouraged. In 1935, when Koen was only 17, she set a national record in the 800-meter race. The talented Koen then took part in the 1936 Berlin Olympics. Unfortunately for Koen, the two following Olympics were canceled due to World War II, but she continued to train and compete. It was during this time that Koen married the Dutch women's track coach, Jan Blankers, and had her first child.

No one expected this new mother to get back into sports, but she did. Not long after the birth of her first child, Koen returned to the track and set six new world track-and-field records. Then, only six weeks after giving birth to her second child, Koen won two gold medals at the 1946 European Championships.

Koen was an athlete, but she was also a conventional wife and mother of the time. She kept the house clean, did the cooking, and took care of her children. She did all of this while training. Her husband supported her athletic career. Many people, however, felt that a married mother should not compete in sports. When Koen decided to leave her children behind and go to London to compete in the 1948 Olympics, many people even in her own country were outraged.

Koen went anyway, and the 1948 London Olympics turned out to be the high point of her career. It was there that this thirty-year-old mother of two became the first woman to win four gold medals in the Olympic Games. She won in every event she was allowed to enter. She might have won more, but the rules still only allowed her to compete in three individual events and one relay.[2] When Koen returned home with her medals, the Dutch had forgiven her. She returned to a hero's welcome. They called her "The Flying Housewife."

Koen proved that a wife and mother could also be a world-class athlete. In fact, the International Association of Athletic Federations named Koen "Female Athlete of the Twentieth Century" in 1999. It's thanks to Fanny Blankers-Koen that twenty-first-century sportswomen of all types are now common, and it's no longer surprising to see someone of Dara Torres's age compete on the world stage.

3

4

5

6

7

---

[2] *relay:* a team race where an object (called a *baton*) is passed from one runner to the next runner

4 READING CHECK

A Are these statements true or false? Write *T* (true) or *F* (false).

1 _____ Dara Torres and Fanny Blankers-Koen were both mothers of young children when they competed in sports.

2 _____ Women have always been allowed to compete in the Olympics.

3 _____ Koen listened to the public and quit sports after she became a mother.

B Circle the letter of the best item to complete each sentence.

1 In 2008, people reacted to Dara Torres competing in the Olympics with _____ .
   a disapproval   **b** acceptance   **c** surprise

2 Fanny Blankers-Koen participated in _____ Olympic Games.
   a one   **b** two   **c** three

3 In the second modern Olympics, women could compete in _____ .
   a all sports that men competed in
   b sports such as archery, golf, and ice-skating
   c some track-and-field events

4 Fanny Blankers-Koen set a record in the 800-meter race in _____ .
   a 1935   **b** 1936   **c** 1946

5 Koen set six world records _____ .
   a after the birth of her first child
   b six weeks after giving birth to her second child
   c at the 1946 European Championships

6 When Koen decided to compete in the 1948 Olympics, people in Holland _____ .
   a were very angry with her
   b supported her decision
   c did not pay attention

7 By 1948, women were allowed to compete in _____ individual events.
   a 4   **b** 3   **c** 5

8 When Koen returned to Holland from London, the Dutch people _____ .
   a welcomed her home
   b ignored her
   c were angry with her

5 VOCABULARY CHECK

A Retell the story. Fill in the blanks with the correct words from the box.

athlete	career	conventional	disapproved
encouraged	participation	set records	society
talented	unacceptable		

Fanny Blankers-Koen was a/an _____ who competed
in track-and-field events in the 1930s and 1940s. During that time,
however, most of _____ thought a mother should lead
a/an _____ life of raising children and taking care of
the house. They thought a mother's _____ in sports was
_____ . Although the public _____ of
Koen's involvement with sports, her family _____ her to
play sports, even after she had children.

Koen was a/an _____ sportswoman, who
_____ in many races. Koen's long _____
as a track-and-field star was finally honored when she won the "Female
Athlete of the Twentieth Century" award in 1999.

B Circle the best word to complete each sentence.

1 The tennis (star / coach / athlete) showed the students how to hit the
ball correctly.

2 The ice-skater wants to (train / coach / compete) in the next
Winter Olympics.

3 Olympic officials no longer (forbid / encourage / allow) women
to participate.

4 She enjoyed (individual / conventional / dangerous) sports such as cycling
or swimming.

5 To be a successful runner, an athlete must (coach / train / study) for many
hours every day.

6 APPLYING READING SKILLS

Making an inference is an important reading skill. It means being able to see what the writer did not explain or state directly. You can make inferences by asking yourself questions when something is not clear.

A Look at the sentence below. It is unclear why the writer wrote "unfortunately." Answer the first three questions so that you can infer the answer to the fourth question.

> "Unfortunately for Koen, the two following Olympics were canceled due to World War II, but she continued to train and compete."

1 How old was Koen during the 1936 Olympics?
2 How old would she have been in the 1940 and 1944 Olympics?
3 Would Koen have done well in the 1940 and 1944 Olympics?

4 Why did the writer write "unfortunately"?

_____

B Answer the following questions.

1 The author writes at the end of paragraph 1 that in 1948 "things were very different for women." The rest of the reading explains this statement, but it never states these differences directly. What do you think they are?
2 In paragraph 2, we read that Olympic officials allowed women to compete in "*some* track-and-field events." Can you infer which types of events they could and could not compete in?
3 In paragraph 4, the author doesn't explain why no one expected Koen to return to sports. Why do you think no one expected this?
4 What was the "hero's welcome" the Dutch gave Koen? (paragraph 6)

7 DISCUSSION

Discuss the following questions in pairs or groups.

1 Do you think Koen deserved to be named "Female Athlete of the Twentieth Century"? Explain.
2 Do you think it is acceptable for mothers of young children to have athletic or other professional careers? Explain.
3 What sports are popular with women today? To watch? To play?

The Big Fish

1 TOPIC PREVIEW

A Some people take on amazing challenges. Read the activities below, and put them in order from 1 to 5, with 1 being the activity you think is the most challenging. Share your answers with your classmates.

_____ climbing Mount Everest

_____ cycling from the East Coast to the West Coast of North America

_____ swimming from England to France

_____ sailing alone across the Atlantic Ocean

_____ walking across Antarctica

B Read the title of this chapter, look at the picture, and discuss the following questions.

1 What is the farthest you have run, swum, biked, walked, or climbed?
2 What challenge do you think the man in the picture is facing?
3 What do you think the reading is going to be about?

2 VOCABULARY PREVIEW

A Read the word lists. Put a check (✓) next to the words that you know and can use in a sentence. Compare your answers with a partner. Then look up any unfamiliar words in a dictionary.

Sports and Fitness	Academic Word List	Environmental Studies
hold (a) **record** **marathon** **pace** (*n.*) **strength**	(raise) **awareness** **equipment** **goal** **mental** **physical**	**deforestation** **oxygen** **pollution** **protect** **rain forest** **threatened** (*adj.*)

The chart shows selected words from the reading related to sports and fitness, environmental studies, and the Academic Word List (AWL). For more information about the AWL, see page 121.

B Write the word from Part A next to its definition.

1 A gas in the air that animals need in order to live: _____

2 Relating to the body: _____

3 The set of objects that are used for a job or activity: _____

4 Damage to water or air by harmful substances: _____

5 Something you want to do successfully in the future: _____

6 The speed at which something happens or is done: _____

7 To maintain the highest or best in an activity: _____

8 The knowledge or understanding of something: _____

9 Having the chance of not surviving: _____

10 A place in a tropical area that is very wet: _____

11 Power and energy: _____

12 When all the trees in a large area are cut down: _____

13 Relating to the mind; involving the process of thinking:

_____

14 To keep someone or something safe from harm: _____

15 A race or activity that continues for a long time: _____

MP3 **3** READING

Preview the questions in Reading Check Part A on page 61. Then read the story.

The Big Fish

Strel in Belém, Brazil

The Amazon River is not a river anyone wants to swim, especially since it's the home of deadly piranhas, anaconda snakes, crocodiles, bull sharks, and dangerous currents. If you're marathon swimmer Martin Strel, however, you look at the powerful Amazon and see a challenge that can't be refused. Using his physical and mental strength, this man swam the largest river on Earth[1] from its starting place in Peru all the way through Brazil to the Atlantic Ocean in 2007. Only a man like Strel could complete this difficult challenge.

Strel is a large, middle-aged man from Slovenia who was raised in a village called Mokronog, which means "wet feet" in English. Strel has always loved swimming. He swam in pools, ponds, and small rivers as a young boy. As he grew older, Strel began swimming in larger rivers and soon became the world's best marathon swimmer. Over the years, Strel has swum through more than 12,000 miles (19,300 kilometers) of the world's longest rivers, from Europe's Danube to China's Yangtze. Strel is a person who likes to swim alone. He needs only the company of the river itself – and the longer the river, the better.

1

2

---

[1] *the largest river on Earth by volume*

3   Though he holds world records for his swims, Strel now swims for peace, friendship, and a clean environment. He talks to audiences about the reasons for his swims. He has swum in dirty rivers to promote the need for clean water. He swam the Amazon to raise people's awareness of the importance of this region. The Amazon Rain Forest produces 20 percent of the world's oxygen, and it is threatened by deforestation and pollution. If Strel could get people to pay attention to the Amazon, he hoped they might want to help protect and save it.

4   All of the rivers in which Strel has swum are difficult, but the Amazon was the most challenging. Its length, amount of water, difficult currents, extreme tides,[2] and dangerous creatures required a large support team and a lot of equipment. A group of doctors and guides traveled with Strel. Strel swam through deadly marine life, feeling the occasional touch of a large unknown creature. He never looked in the water to see what it was. He just kept swimming, determined to reach his goal.

5   Along the way, Strel made friends with local people. As he swam down the river, large crowds came out to see him. People around the world also followed Strel's progress through news reports. The world was watching both Strel and the Amazon.

6   Although Strel had the support of his team and his fans, his biggest challenge was a mental one. He had to calm his mind as he spent ten hours a day alone in the water, swimming from port to port. All he heard was his steady breath and the sound of his arms in the water. He filled the hours with dreams of his family. When he pulled into a port he would swim steadily, not hesitating in his pace. He could hear the noise of the cheering crowd, but he wouldn't look at his fans until he had reached the bank. Then he would raise his arms and smile.

7   After 3,274 miles (5,269 kilometers) and 66 days on the river, fighting nature and solitude, Strel finally arrived in Belém, Brazil, where the Amazon meets the Atlantic. When he touched land, he was 26 pounds lighter and smiling with relief. He had become the first person to swim the Amazon. He had also achieved his other goal. He had built cross-cultural friendships and helped the world think about this environmentally important region.

---

[2] *tide:* the regular rising and falling of the sea level

4 READING CHECK

A Circle the letter of the best answer.

1 Why does Martin Strel swim in big rivers?
  a to compete against other swimmers
  b to become famous
  c to raise awareness about peace, friendship, and the environment

2 Why was the Amazon River the most difficult river for Strel to swim?
  a Strel had no help.
  b The Amazon was dirty.
  c The Amazon had dangerous currents and creatures.

3 What was Strel's biggest challenge in swimming the Amazon River?
  a to stay calm
  b to lose weight
  c to increase his pace

B Are these statements true or false? Write *T* (true) or *F* (false).

1 _____ Martin Strel learned to swim in the ocean.

2 _____ Strel prefers the company of other swimmers to swimming alone.

3 _____ Strel has swum the Danube and Yangtze Rivers.

4 _____ Strel has never held a world record for his swims.

5 _____ The Amazon region is no longer threatened by deforestation.

6 _____ Strel felt marine life touch him while he swam the Amazon.

7 _____ No one had heard of Strel's Amazon swim until after he completed it.

8 _____ Strel swam 12 hours a day in the Amazon River.

9 _____ While Strel swam, he thought of his family.

10 _____ Strel swam the Amazon River for 26 days and lost 66 pounds.

5 VOCABULARY CHECK

A Retell the story. Fill in the blanks with the correct words from the box.

awareness	equipment	holds records	marathon	mental
oxygen	pace	physical	rain forest	strength

_____ swimmer Martin Strel _____

1   2

for swimming many of the world's greatest rivers. Strel's

amazing _____ is both _____

3   4

and _____ and helps him to keep his steady

5

_____ . In addition, Strel's _____ , such

6   7

as swim gear, charts, and medical supplies, as well as a support team, help

him during his long swims.

Because the tropical _____ supplies 20 percent of the

8

world's _____ , Strel thought swimming the Amazon

9

would raise a/an _____ of the environmental problems of

10

this region. Indeed, his successful swim has gotten the public to notice this

region of the world!

B Write a short paragraph about environmental problems. Use the following
words: *deforestation, goal, pollution, protect,* and *threatened.*

_____

_____

_____

_____

_____

_____

_____

6 APPLYING READING SKILLS

Using reference materials, such as atlases, encyclopedias, and Web sites, after you read is sometimes necessary to get the most complete understanding of a reading.

A Look at this map of South America. Find the following places that are mentioned in the reading. Put each number in the correct place on the map.

1 Peru

2 Brazil

3 the Atlantic Ocean

4 the start of the Amazon

5 Belém, the place where the Amazon meets the Atlantic

6 the Amazon Rain Forest

B Use reference materials to answer the following questions.

1 What type of animal is a piranha?

2 What type of animal is an anaconda?

3 Which countries have borders with Slovenia?

4 In which country does the Danube River begin? What are three other countries that it goes through?

5 In which city does the Yangtze River end?

7 DISCUSSION

Discuss the following questions in pairs or groups.

1 Strel swam the Amazon to raise awareness of pollution in the Amazon. What other kinds of activities have people done to raise awareness of environmental problems?

2 Strel also swam the Amazon for the physical and mental challenge. What type of physical or mental challenge would you like to accomplish in the future?

Blade Runner

1 TOPIC PREVIEW

A Look at the names below. These people have something in common. Put a check (✓) next to the people you have heard of. Do you know what they have in common? Share your answers with your classmates.

1 _____ Andrea Bocelli

2 _____ Stephen Hawking

3 _____ Helen Keller

4 _____ Yitzhak Perlman

5 _____ Ludwig van Beethoven

6 _____ Stevie Wonder

B Read the title of this chapter, look at the picture, and discuss the following questions.

1 Do you know people who have physical problems but who still have accomplished great things? Explain.

2 What is the man in the picture doing? What is different about him?

3 What do you think the reading is going to be about?

2 VOCABULARY PREVIEW

A Read the word lists. Put a check (✓) next to the words that you know and can use in a sentence. Compare your answers with a partner. Then look up any unfamiliar words in a dictionary.

Sports and Fitness	Academic Word List	Biomedical Engineering
able-bodied disabled excel obstacle qualify sprinter	device flexibility injury recovery specifically	artificial blade prosthesis wheelchair

The chart shows selected words from the reading related to sports and fitness, biomedical engineering, and the Academic Word List (AWL). For more information about the AWL, see page 121.

B Fill in the blanks with words from Part A.

1 When you are extremely good at something, you _____ at it.

2 The doctor used a special _____ to fix the patient's bone.

3 The directions _____ said to turn left, not right.

4 The girl used a/an _____ because she couldn't walk.

5 The _____ of this knife can cut very thin slices of bread.

6 _____ people can still achieve great things.

7 The biggest _____ in the race was the cold weather.

8 The runner who had no legs had _____ legs instead.

9 Doctors gave the woman a/an _____ for her missing arm.

10 The best _____ won the short race.

11 The man suffered a head _____ in the accident.

12 The woman's _____ took about a month. Then she felt better.

13 _____ people usually don't need physical help.

14 The young man improved his _____ by practicing yoga.

15 To _____ for the finals, she had to win five games.

Preview the questions in Reading Check Part A on page 68. Then read the story.

Blade Runner

1   It's race day. A young
athlete walks onto the track
and takes his place next
to the other runners. The
starting gun fires, and the
young athlete begins to run.
As the group races down
the track, the crowd begins
to cheer. The young athlete
passes the first runner.
Then he passes another, and
yet another. The finish line
comes near, and the young
athlete rushes forward with
great speed. He crosses the
finish line to the loud roar of the crowd. Who is this young athlete?
He is South African sprinter Oscar Pistorius. Why is the crowd
cheering so loudly? Pistorius has two artificial legs, and he has won
the race against able-bodied runners.

Oscar Pistorius

2   Oscar Pistorius was born with the determination and talent of
a world-class sprinter. However, young Oscar had a great obstacle.
When Oscar was born, he was missing the calf bone[1] in each leg.
Doctors gave his parents two choices. One choice was that doctors
could amputate[2] their son's lower legs and give the boy artificial legs,
or prostheses. The other choice was that Pistorius could spend his life
in a wheelchair. His parents decided on giving him prostheses. With
these artificial legs, he could learn to walk. There was one thing his
parents never expected, however. Their son would not only walk, but
he would also become an extraordinary track star.

3   From a young age, Pistorius excelled at sports even with his
artificial legs. He competed in tennis, soccer, water polo, and rugby.
Then in 2004 at the age of 18, Pistorius received a knee injury. As part
of the recovery process, he started running. Soon he was running not

---

[1] *calf bone:* a bone located in the front of the lower leg
[2] *amputate:* to cut off someone's arm, leg, finger, etc., during a medical operation

just well, but incredibly fast. In that same year, he decided to become a competitive sprinter. He then went to the Athens Paralympics,[3] where he set four world sprinting records and won four gold medals.

How did Pistorius become such a remarkable sprinter so quickly? He was a determined natural athlete, and he had the help of his prostheses: the Cheetah Flex Foot.[4] The Cheetah Flex Foot is designed to help athletes like Pistorius sprint. It is a blade shaped like the letter "j" and has the flexibility of a natural foot and ankle. It allows a runner to sprint much like an able-bodied runner.

4

Nicknamed "Blade Runner," Pistorius continued to break records in Paralympic competitions. In 2007, he achieved something extraordinary. He won the silver medal for the 400-meter race in the South African National Championships. He had won against *able-bodied* men! Now he thought it might be possible that he could achieve his dream of competing in the 2008 Summer Olympics in Beijing.

5

In early 2008, however, the International Association of Athletics Federations (IAAF) ruled that they would not allow Pistorius to compete in the Summer Olympics. The committee claimed the Cheetahs gave the disabled sprinter more power. Pistorius and many others disagreed. Pistorius challenged the ruling, and he was given permission to compete just months before the Summer Olympics. He tried out for the South African Olympic Team but missed qualifying for the team by less than a second. Although he did not meet his Olympic goal, Pistorius still went on to win a gold medal in the 100-, 200-, and 400-meter races at the Paralympics that same year.

6

Pistorius would have been the first amputee in the Olympics to use a device specifically designed to help him in his sport. Although the IAAF finally allowed Pistorius to try out for the Olympics, that doesn't mean all disabled athletes with special prostheses will be able to participate in future Olympics. In the future, the IAAF will still examine each disabled athlete's case. Pistorius's determination and success, however, have given hope to millions of other disabled athletes. Perhaps there will be a day when the crowd cheers for disabled athletes with prosthetic devices as they compete in the Olympics next to their able-bodied competitors.

7

---

[3] *Paralympics:* Olympics for the disabled
[4] *Cheetah Flex Foot:* named after the cheetah, the fastest land mammal

4 READING CHECK

A Are these statements true or false? Write *T* (true) or *F* (false).

1 _____ Oscar Pistorius was born without calf bones.

2 _____ Oscar Pistorius had been a sprinter for years when he won his first race.

3 _____ Oscar Pistorius races against both disabled and able-bodied runners.

B Answer the questions with information from the reading.

1 Who is Oscar Pistorius?

_____

2 What were the choices Pistorius's doctor gave to his parents? Which one did they choose?

_____

3 Why did his parents make their choice?

_____

4 Why did Pistorius begin running?

_____

5 What helped Pistorius achieve success, in addition to his natural talent?

_____

6 What was extraordinary about Pistorius's 2007 success?

_____

7 Why did the International Association of Athletics Federations not want to allow Pistorius to compete in the 2008 Olympics?

_____

8 Why didn't Pistorius compete in the 2008 Olympics?

_____

5 VOCABULARY CHECK

A Retell the story. Fill in the blanks with the correct words from the box.

able-bodied	artificial	blade	device
disabled	excelled	obstacle	prostheses
sprinter	wheelchair		

Oscar Pistorius was born without calf bones in his lower legs. Instead of spending his life in a/an _____ , his parents

1

decided to give their son _____ . With the help of these

2

_____ legs, Pistorius _____ at sports.

3 4

Pistorius began to run after he was hurt playing rugby. He was so fast on the track that he decided to become a/an _____ .

5

He no longer faced the _____ of having no legs. The

6

Cheetah Flex Foot, a/an _____ that looks like a

7

j-shaped _____ , soon allowed Pistorius to become the

8

fastest man without real legs. Even though Pistorius is considered a/an

_____ runner because of his missing legs, he runs

9

alongside and often beats _____ runners.

10

B Fill in the blanks with the correct words. Use the correct verb tense or the correct singular or plural noun form.

Verb	Noun	Adjective
flex	flexibility	flexible
injure	injury	injured
qualify	qualification	qualified
recover	recovery	recovered
specify	specification	specific

1 The team doctor says the star player will _____ soon.

2 Athletes have to be _____ in order to move so easily.

3 Football players often _____ themselves during practice.

4 The runner met the minimum _____ and can compete.

5 There are _____ rules that players must follow.

6 APPLYING READING SKILLS

Organizing information into a chart can help you deepen your understanding of a reading and see how different parts of the reading relate to each other. It can also help you write a short summary of the reading, which can be useful if you have to prepare for a test on it.

A Fill in the chart with information from the reading. One example for each column has been done for you.

OSCAR PISTORIUS		
His mental and physical characteristics	**His major achievements**	**His challenges (past and present)**
amputee – no legs below the knee	*excelled at sports from a young age*	*born without a calf bone in each leg*

B Use the information from the chart to write a short summary of "Blade Runner."

_____

_____

_____

_____

_____

_____

7 DISCUSSION

Discuss the following questions in pairs or groups.

1 Do you know anyone who is disabled, has a prosthesis, or is in a wheelchair and also plays sports? Explain.

2 Do you think Pistorius's special Cheetah Flex Feet give him an advantage over able-bodied athletes?

3 Do you think disabled or able-bodied athletes should be allowed to use special devices or expensive equipment when they compete? Explain.

VOCABULARY REVIEW

Chapter **7**	Chapter **8**	Chapter **9**
Sports and Fitness	**Sports and Fitness**	**Sports and Fitness**
athlete · coach (*n.*) · compete · set (a) record · talented · train (*v.*)	hold (a) record · marathon · pace (*n.*) · strength	able-bodied · disabled · excel · obstacle · qualify · sprinter
Academic Word List	**Academic Word List**	**Academic Word List**
conventional · individual (*adj.*) · participation	(raise) awareness · equipment · goal · mental · physical	device · flexibility · injury · recovery · specifically
Sociology	**Environmental Studies**	**Biomedical Engineering**
career · disapprove (of) · encourage · forbid · society · unacceptable	deforestation · oxygen · pollution · protect · rain forest · threatened (*adj.*)	artificial · blade · prosthesis · wheelchair

Find words in the chart that match the definitions. Answers to 1–4 are from Chapter 7. Answers to 5–8 are from Chapter 8. Answers to 9–12 are from Chapter 9.

1 Behaving or thinking in a usual way: _____

2 To tell someone that they are not allowed to do something: _____

3 To take part in a sports event and try to win: _____

4 To think that something or someone is bad, wrong: _____

5 The speed at which something happens or is done: _____

6 The set of objects that are used for a job or activity: _____

7 To keep someone or something safe from harm: _____

8 Power and energy: _____

9 Not natural; made by people: _____

10 The skill or ability to bend or change easily: _____

11 To achieve a very high level of knowledge or skill: _____

12 The process of getting better after an illness or injury: _____

VOCABULARY IN USE

Work with a partner or small group, and discuss the questions below.

1 When you were younger, what did your parents or teachers **encourage** you to do?

2 What kinds of **obstacles** do women still face in the working world?

3 If you could choose any **career** or change your current career, what would it be?

4 Do you think professional **athletes** should be paid high salaries? Explain.

5 How can cross-cultural **awareness** help international relations?

6 What kinds of things can a person do to **train** to run a **marathon**?

7 What does **society** do to help **disabled** people? Explain.

8 What is one thing you **excel** at? Explain.

ROLE PLAY

Work with a partner. One student is a newspaper reporter. The other student is an athlete – for example, a runner, a swimmer, or a soccer player – who has just won an important race or game.

Reporter: Prepare general questions to ask the athlete about how he or she trained for the event and about any obstacles he or she faced during the event.

Athlete: Prepare a list of how you trained for the event and about any obstacles you faced during the event.

WRITING

Imagine that you are Fanny Blankers-Koen, Martin Strel, or Oscar Pistorius. You have been asked by the local high school to share your story with students. Write an article for the school newspaper, answering the following questions.

- What have been some challenges in your athletic career?

- How have you overcome these challenge?

- What has been your biggest accomplishment? What did you learn from it?

WEBQUEST

Find more information about the topics in this unit by going on the Internet. Go to www.cambridge.org/readthis and follow the instructions for doing a WebQuest. Search for facts. Have fun. Good luck!

UNIT

4

Political Science

Chapter **10**

Cyrus the Great

Why do we still remember a king who ruled 2,500 years ago?

Content areas:
- Political Science
- History

Chapter **11**

A Famous Work of Art Finds Its Home

A modern work of art sends a powerful message to the world.

Content areas:
- Political Science
- Art

Chapter **12**

The Power of the Media

Two young journalists discover a crime at the highest levels of government.

Content areas:
- Political Science
- Journalism

CHAPTER
10
Cyrus the Great

1 TOPIC PREVIEW

A Imagine that you can travel back in time 2,500 years. Put a check (✓) next to the things you might find. Share your answers with your classmates.

1 _____ soldiers fighting

2 _____ glass windows

3 _____ people working in fields

4 _____ walled cities

5 _____ _____ (your idea)

B Read the title of this chapter, look at the picture, and discuss the following questions.

1 Who do you think the man in the picture is? Where is he? Explain.
2 What do you think were characteristics of a great leader 2,500 years ago?
3 What do you think the reading is going to be about?

2 VOCABULARY PREVIEW

A Read the word lists. Put a check (✓) next to the words that you know and can use in a sentence. Compare your answers with a partner. Then look up any unfamiliar words in a dictionary.

Political Science	Academic Word List	History
defeat (*v.*)	conflict (*n.*)	conquer
govern	(on) display	historian
(in) power	document (*n.*)	kingdom
(have) rights	policy	slave
take control	principle	
	stability	

The chart shows selected words from the reading related to political science, history, and the Academic Word List (AWL). For more information about the AWL, see page 121.

B Fill in the blanks with words from Part A.

1 The _____ enjoyed studying and writing about the past.

2 Ancient objects are on _____ in the museum.

3 A _____ between two nations caused the war.

4 The government's _____ helped the people to feel safe.

5 The ruler wanted to _____ the land and rule the people.

6 The king wrote a _____ giving all his people freedom.

7 A good leader believes in the _____ of treating people fairly.

8 A person who is owned by another person is called a _____ .

9 When the king died, he had been in _____ for 50 years.

10 The people were happy with their country's new economic

_____ .

11 The king tried to _____ his enemies and destroy their land.

12 Freedom of religion and speech are important _____ .

13 The ruler did not _____ well, so he lost his power.

14 The king was kind, so the people in his _____ were happy.

15 The government wanted to _____ of the banks.

Preview the questions in Reading Check Part A on page 78. Then read the story.

Cyrus the Great

1   In 1879, archeologists[1] digging
through dirt in the hot sun in Iraq made
a surprising discovery. They found an
ancient clay cylinder[2] with writing on
it. When experts examined the cylinder,
they discovered the words of a king
who had ruled the Persian Empire[3]
2,500 years earlier. Many people now
believe these words are the world's first
document about human rights. Who
was this king, and what are these
human rights?

The Cyrus Cylinder

2   In ancient times, kings ruled by fear.
When they defeated a village, they
typically burned the houses and fields.
The conquered people became prisoners
and sometimes slaves. These people had
no rights. They had to follow the religion of the new king and obey him
or risk terrible punishment. Historians thought this was true for all
kings until they found the cylinder.

3   The cylinder told them of a different kind of king. This king was
Cyrus the Great. Cyrus was born in the fifth century BCE, in the
mountain grasslands of Persia. At first, Cyrus ruled a small kingdom,
but later his excellent military and political skills helped him to form
the largest empire of his time.

4   Cyrus was different from other rulers because he conquered many
lands without much fighting. He was also good at creating stability.
During his first conflict, Cyrus came to an agreement with his
enemy's leaders so that few lives would be lost. After winning the
conflict, Cyrus did not burn down the villages. Instead, he surprised
the leaders by giving them jobs and asking some of them to help

---

[1] *archeologist:* a person who studies ancient cultures by examining their buildings,
tools, and other objects

[2] *cylinder:* a solid object that has long straight sides and circular ends of equal size

[3] *Persian Empire:* an area of land that included modern-day Iran and Iraq

govern the villages and farmlands. More importantly, Cyrus did not force the people to make major changes in their religion or culture. In this way, he was able to win the trust of the people, and this helped strengthen his kingdom.

Cyrus's most famous conquest was the powerful city of Babylon. In contrast to the simple mountain world that Cyrus had come from, Babylon was a wealthy and powerful city. The king of Babylon enjoyed a comfortable life in a royal palace. His palace and the city were surrounded and protected by high walls. Soldiers guarded the walls and prevented anyone from climbing over them. The Euphrates River flowed under the walls, bringing valuable water to the people and the farmlands. Therefore, no one needed to leave the city. It was also difficult for anyone, including enemies, to enter the city. 5

Since he could not knock down the walls of Babylon, Cyrus came up with a different plan to take over the city. He told his engineers to dig channels[4] to change the flow of the Euphrates. Late at night, he and his men directed the water of the river into the channels. Soon the river was only knee-deep. The men were then able to walk through the shallow water under the walls of the city. Cyrus and his men easily took control of Babylon. When he woke up the next morning, the king of Babylon was shocked to learn that he was no longer in power. 6

The next day, Cyrus declared himself the king of Babylon. He created principles for a new government. First, he gave the conquered people their freedom. Second, he gave the Babylonians the right to follow their own religions and cultures. Finally, he promised to rebuild their homes and temples. These are the human rights that are written on the Cyrus Cylinder. 7

The Cyrus Cylinder is now on display in the British Museum in London. A copy is in the United Nations building in New York. The human rights on the cylinder have been translated into the six official languages used by the UN. Today, Cyrus's beliefs about human rights still influence the policies of many of the world's leaders. 8

---

[4] *channel:* a passage that water can flow along

4 READING CHECK

A Are these statements true or false? Write *T* (true) or *F* (false).

1 _____ Cyrus the Great was a Greek ruler.

2 _____ Cyrus the Great took control of the city of Babylon.

3 _____ Cyrus the Great believed in human rights for conquered people.

B Circle the letter of the best answer.

1 When did Cyrus the Great live?
   a in 1879   **b** 2,500 years ago   **c** 25,000 years ago

2 Where did archeologists find the Cyrus Cylinder?
   a in Iraq   **b** in Great Britain   **c** in Iran

3 What did Cyrus do during his first conflict with another army?
   a He killed his enemy's leaders.
   b He captured the other army in the middle of the night.
   c He came to an agreement with his enemy's leaders.

4 How did Cyrus create stability after winning a conflict?
   a He scared people so that they obeyed his rules.
   b He made people follow one religion.
   c He allowed people to keep their homes and culture.

5 How was Babylon different from the land where Cyrus had come from?
   a It was a simple mountain grassland.
   b It was a wealthy and powerful city.
   c It was a small village.

6 How did Cyrus capture Babylon?
   a He went over the wall that surrounded the city.
   b He went under the wall that surrounded the city.
   c The slaves inside the city let him in.

7 What did Cyrus do after he conquered Babylon?
   a He gave the king freedom and told him to leave Babylon.
   b He gave the conquered people their freedom.
   c He did not change anything in Babylon.

8 Where is the original Cyrus Cylinder today?
   a in the British Museum
   b in the United Nations
   c in Iraq

5 VOCABULARY CHECK

A Retell the story. Fill in the blanks with the correct words from the box.

conflicts	display	historians	kingdom	policies
power	principles	rights	slaves	took control

Some _____ believe that the first document stating that
                        1
conquered people should have human _____ was written
                                    2
2,500 years ago by Cyrus the Great. It was written on a cylinder that is now
on _____ at the British Museum in London.
      3

Cyrus ruled a small _____ in ancient Persia. He was a kind
                     4
ruler, and his leadership skills helped him to form the largest empire of
the land. For example, after he _____ of Babylon, he created
                                5
_____ that were guidelines for a new government. He did not
      6
make people _____ , and he gave jobs to the leaders. There
            7
were very few _____ while Cyrus was in _____ .
              8   9

Cyrus's beliefs in the fair treatment of conquered people continue today
with the _____ of many of our world leaders.
           10

B Fill in the blanks with the correct word. Use the correct verb tense or the correct
singular or plural noun form.

Verb	Noun	Adjective
conquer	conqueror	conquered
defeat	defeat	defeated
document	document	documented
govern	government	governmental
stabilize	stability	stable

1 The new leader _____ the country's failing economy.

2 The Declaration of Independence is an important U.S. _____ .

3 People often disagree with their _____ when it raises taxes.

4 The country's _____ of its enemies happened very quickly.

5 Alexander the Great and Kublai Khan were both ancient _____ .

6 APPLYING READING SKILLS

*Good writers support their main ideas with supporting details. Good readers are skilled at **finding main ideas and supporting details**.*

A Write *M* next to the two sentences that are main ideas. Write *S* next to the sentences that give supporting details. Match the *S* sentences to the *M* sentences they support.

1 _____ In ancient times, most kings ruled by fear.

2 _____ He did not force the people to change their religion or culture.

3 _____ Cyrus created new principles of government.

4 _____ They did not give the conquered people any rights.

5 _____ He gave the conquered people their freedom.

6 _____ They typically burned the villages and farmlands.

B Find two details from the text that support each main idea.

MAIN IDEA	SUPPORTING DETAILS
1 Cyrus was different from other rulers.	
2 Babylon was a wealthy and powerful city.	
3 The Cyrus Cylinder contains an important historical document.	

7 DISCUSSION

Discuss the following questions in pairs or groups.

1 What basic human rights do you think that all people today should have?

2 What do you think are characteristics of great military leaders today?

3 What rights do you think military leaders should give to prisoners of war?

A Famous Work of Art Finds Its Home

1 TOPIC PREVIEW

A What do you think Picasso was thinking about when he created the painting *Guernica*? Put a check (✓) next to your answers. Share your answers with your classmates.

1 _____ birth

2 _____ death

3 _____ happiness

4 _____ anger

5 _____ violence

6 _____ _____ (your idea)

B Read the title of this chapter, look at the picture, and discuss the following questions.

1 What do you know about Picasso and modern art?

2 Look at the picture *Guernica*. What do you see in the painting? How does it make you feel? Explain.

3 What do you think the reading is going to be about?

2 VOCABULARY PREVIEW

A Read the word lists. Put a check (✓) next to the words that you know and can use in a sentence. Compare your answers with a partner. Then look up any unfamiliar words in a dictionary.

Political Science	Academic Word List	Art
activist	affect (v.)	canvas
democratically	controversial	inspired (adj.)
dictator	exhibit (v.)	masterpiece
elected (adj.)	liberate	sensation
resistance	reaction	
	symbol	

The chart shows selected words from the reading related to political science, art, and the Academic Word List (AWL). For more information about the AWL, see page 121.

B Write the word from Part A next to its definition.

1 The cloth an artist paints on: _____

2 A feeling or an action in response to something else: _____

3 Causing or likely to cause a disagreement: _____

4 Someone who rules a country with complete power: _____

5 Chosen for a political office: _____

6 Done in a way so that government represents the people:

_____

7 To show something in public: _____

8 To free someone or something from control: _____

9 One thing used to represent another thing: _____

10 Something that causes great excitement or interest: _____

11 Influenced or motivated by someone or something: _____

12 A work of art made with great skill or talent: _____

13 To have an influence on someone or something: _____

14 A person who tries to create social or political change: _____

15 A fight against or opposition to someone or something: _____

Preview the questions in Reading Check Part A on page 85. Then read the story.

A Famous Work of Art Finds Its Home

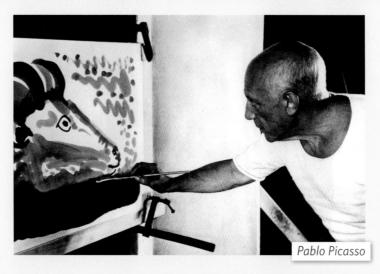

Pablo Picasso

One sunny morning in 1937, the small village of Guernica in northern Spain was crowded with people enjoying market day. Suddenly, something terrible happened. German military planes appeared overhead, dropping bombs[1] on the village below. Many people and animals were instantly injured or killed.

The democratically elected government of Spain was fighting in a civil war[2] against a military leader named Francisco Franco. It was Franco who had asked Germany to bomb Guernica.

At that time, Pablo Picasso, a well-known artist from Spain, was living in Paris. A few days after the attack, Picasso saw the newspapers. On the front pages were large black-and-white photographs of the death and destruction in Guernica. The suffering of these people from his country affected Picasso deeply.

Picasso became a political activist for Spain during the Spanish Civil War. He decided to create a painting about the bombing of Guernica to exhibit at the World's Fair in Paris that year. He knew that many people would come to the fair. He hoped the painting would make visitors think, talk, and be inspired to do something to help Spain.

1

2

3

4

---

[1] *bomb:* a weapon made of exploding material

[2] *civil war:* a war fought between groups of people living in the same country

5   Picasso used a large canvas, which covered an entire wall of the Spanish exhibit at the fair. He used only black and white paint because of his strong reaction to the black-and-white newspaper photographs. He showed the tragedies[3] of war by painting a suffering mother and child, a dying soldier, a horse twisted in pain, and a bull[4] Picasso used the horse to represent the Spanish people and the bull to represent violence and darkness. His finished painting was titled *Guernica*.

6   *Guernica* immediately created a sensation. The painting was powerful, but it was not pretty. Some people hated it. They said it was not art because art should be beautiful. Other people loved the painting. They said it was art just like any other painting because it was about human experience. This disagreement led to many discussions about art and politics.

7   Meanwhile, *Guernica* became an important symbol of the Spanish resistance to Franco's army. *Guernica* was sent to major cities in Europe, and people paid to see it. The money was given to the soldiers fighting against Franco. During World War II, Picasso sent *Guernica* to the United States to keep it safe. The painting continued to travel throughout the United States and South America for the next 40 years. Art students studied it, and art historians wrote about it. *Guernica* became one of the most controversial paintings in the world.

8   Franco's army won the civil war and helped Franco become a dictator in Spain. Franco asked Picasso to bring *Guernica* to Spain. Picasso refused. He said it could not go to Spain until Spain was liberated from Franco's dictatorship. Unfortunately, Picasso died in 1973 before that could happen.

9   Two years later Franco died, and soon after that, Spain held elections and democracy returned. The Museum of Modern Art in New York, where *Guernica* was being held, respected Picasso's wishes and sent *Guernica* to Spain in 1981. The painting was finally home.

10   Today, *Guernica* hangs in the Reina Sophia Museum in Madrid, where it is well protected. People from all over the world come to see this masterpiece. The civil war is long over in Spain, but the memory of the small, peaceful village and the tragedies of war live on in this famous and controversial work of art.

---

[3] *tragedy:* a very sad event or situation, especially one that involves death or suffering
[4] *bull:* adult male animal of the cattle family

4 READING CHECK

A Circle the letter of the best answer.

1 What is Guernica?
   a a village and a painting
   b an artist and a city
   c a type of airplane and a painting

2 Who was Francisco Franco?
   a a dictator
   b a Spanish artist
   c a democratically elected president

3 What happened in Spain in the late 1930s?
   a Picasso moved back to Spain.
   b the World's Fair
   c a civil war

B Are these statements true or false? Write *T* (true) or *F* (false).

1 _____ Picasso lived in Guernica, Spain.

2 _____ German military planes bombed Guernica in 1937.

3 _____ Picasso became a political activist during the Spanish Civil War.

4 _____ Picasso agreed with Franco and wanted him to win the civil war.

5 _____ Picasso painted *Guernica* in Paris for the World's Fair.

6 _____ *Guernica* is a very small painting.

7 _____ *Guernica* raised money to help Spanish soldiers fight against Franco.

8 _____ Picasso did not allow *Guernica* to leave Europe while he was alive.

9 _____ Picasso asked Franco to bring the painting back to Spain.

10 _____ Franco died before Picasso died.

11 _____ Spain had a democratically elected government after Franco died.

12 _____ *Guernica* is now in the Museum of Modern Art in New York City.

5 VOCABULARY CHECK

A Retell the story. Fill in the blanks with the correct words from the box.

activist	canvas	controversial	democratically	dictator
exhibited	inspired	liberated	masterpiece	sensation

In 1937, Spain was in the middle of a civil war. Francisco Franco was a general fighting against the _____ elected government.
₁ Picasso, a Spanish artist, was living in Paris at the time. When he heard the news that the small Spanish village of Guernica had been bombed by German military planes, he became a political _____
₂ against Franco and his army. He was _____ to make a
₃ political painting about the bombing.

Picasso titled his painting *Guernica*. It was painted on a large
_____ and was _____ for the
₄ ₅
first time at the World's Fair in Paris. The painting created a/an
_____ . Some people said *Guernica* was not art, and the
₆
painting became very _____ .
₇

Guernica traveled through Europe and the United States, but Picasso did not want it to go to Spain until his country was free. In the meantime, Franco had won the war and had become a/an _____
₈
in Spain. When Franco died in 1975, Spain was _____ .
₉
Finally, *Guernica* was sent to Spain, where people from all over the world today can view Picasso's _____ .
₁₀

B Many nouns and verbs are used with specific prepositions, such as *at, by, for, in, of, on,* and *to.* Fill in the blanks with the correct prepositions.

1 Picasso supported the resistance _____ Francisco Franco.

2 People were deeply affected _____ Picasso's painting.

3 Some people had a negative reaction _____ the painting.

4 In a democracy, leaders are elected _____ the people.

5 The bull in *Guernica* was a symbol _____ violence.

6 APPLYING READING SKILLS

> **Understanding the order of events** in a reading means that you know what happens first, second, third, and so on. Making a time line is an excellent way to help you keep track of the order of events.

A Write the letter of the following events into the time line in the correct order.

a Picasso painted *Guernica* for the World's Fair in Paris.
b *Guernica* traveled to the United States.
c German military planes bombed the city of Guernica.
d *Guernica* went to Spain for the first time.
e Pablo Picasso died.
f Democracy returned to Spain.

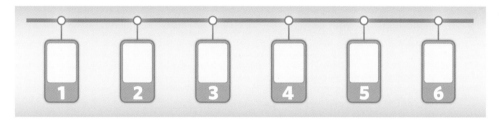

B Circle the correct word for each sentence. Use information from your time line in Part A.

1 Picasso painted *Guernica* (before / after) the bombing in the Spanish village.
2 *Guernica* was in the World's Fair (before / after) it traveled to the United States.
3 *Guernica* traveled to Spain (before / after) Picasso died.
4 Democracy returned to Spain (before / after) *Guernica* traveled to Spain.

7 DISCUSSION

Discuss the following questions in pairs or groups.

1 Look back at the picture of *Guernica* on page 81. Does the painting look different to you than it did the first time you looked at it? Explain.
2 Do you think that *Guernica* is still controversial today? Explain.
3 What types of painting or art do you like? Explain.

The Power of the Media

1 TOPIC PREVIEW

A The news media, such as newspapers, magazines, radio, and television, can have a powerful effect on society. Put a check (✓) next to the effects you think the media can have. Share your answers with your classmates.

1 _____ changing people's opinions about important issues

2 _____ changing the result of a world event

3 _____ destroying a politician's or a celebrity's life or career

4 _____ creating new cultural ideas

5 _____ _____ (your idea)

B Read the title of this chapter, look at the picture, and discuss the following questions.

1 How powerful do you think the media is in the country where you live? Explain.

2 Describe what is happening in this picture. Who is this man? What do you know about him?

3 What do you think the reading is going to be about?

2 VOCABULARY PREVIEW

A Read the word lists. Put a check (✓) next to the words that you know and can use in a sentence. Compare your answers with a partner. Then look up any unfamiliar words in a dictionary.

Political Science	Academic Word List	Journalism
campaign (*n.*)		
candidate	evidence	
headquarters	illegal	article
impeach	investigate	cover (*v.*)
political party	publish	report (*v.*)
resign	source	
term (of office)		

The chart shows selected words from the reading related to political science, journalism, and the Academic Word List (AWL). For more information about the AWL, see page 121.

B Fill in the blanks with words from Part A.

1 The journalist wanted to _____ only political events.

2 A U.S. president can serve more than one _____ of office.

3 The country wanted to _____ its president because he had lied.

4 Which _____ do you want to be president?

5 The detectives needed to _____ the crime in order to solve it.

6 The company _____ are located in Seoul, South Korea.

7 She wanted to _____ from her new job after one week.

8 He agreed to be a/an _____ of information for the news story.

9 He was fired from his job because he did something _____ .

10 The magazine would not _____ the writer's story.

11 Each _____ wants to have the most people in government.

12 He began his _____ for president a year before the election.

13 The police didn't have enough _____ to arrest the suspect.

14 The journalist wrote a great _____ about political crimes.

15 Local TV was the first to _____ the details of the accident.

Preview the questions in Reading Check Part A on page 92. Then read the story.

The Power of the Media

1   Something was not quite right at the Watergate Hotel in Washington, D.C. It was June of 1972, an election year in the United States. Most of the media were focused on the campaigns of the two political parties: the Democrats and the Republicans. They did not pay much attention to the arrest of five burglars[1] who broke into a fifth-floor room of the hotel. However, two young reporters who covered the story noticed some unusual details in the documents from the police.

Bernstein (left) and Woodward

The burglars were well dressed, they had a lot of money with them, and they were able to get help from the city's top lawyers. In addition, the room they broke into was the Democratic Party's national headquarters. Who were these men? Why were they there?

2   Bob Woodward and Carl Bernstein, the two reporters, decided to investigate the crime. Richard Nixon was the U.S. president at the time. He was a Republican, and he wanted a second term of office. Woodward and Bernstein wondered if the burglars were trying to help Nixon's campaign by secretly listening to Democratic Party meetings.

3   The Committee to Re-elect the President (CREEP) was working for Nixon. When Woodward and Bernstein discovered that one of the burglars worked for CREEP, they wrote an article. Their article reported that the burglars had planned to put equipment in the hotel room to record the Democrats' conversations. This article appeared in *The Washington Post*, one of the country's leading newspapers.

4   Many people connected to Nixon became angry with *The Washington Post*. They wanted the newspaper to stop publishing

---

[1] *burglar:* a person who forces his or her way illegally into a house or building, usually to steal things

articles about the Watergate burglary. Other people became important sources for Woodward and Bernstein. These people shared some of the president's secrets, but they said the information was "off the record." That meant that Woodward and Bernstein could not use the sources' names in their articles.

Meanwhile, the campaigns of the political parties continued. The Democratic Party's candidate was George McGovern, but he did not do very well. Nixon easily won the election, and he started his second term of office as president in the winter of 1973.

5

Woodward and Bernstein did not give up. A new source agreed to tell them what he knew about CREEP's activities. However, the source asked them to keep his name a secret. In fact, it was one of Washington's longest- and best-kept secrets for the next 33 years. With his help, the reporters eventually published a front-page story connecting the Watergate burglary to the White House. The public was now angry about this information.

6

Finally, the Federal Bureau of Investigation (FBI) got involved. It learned that the president recorded his conversations, and it asked for the tapes as evidence. Several of Nixon's advisors tried to protect him, but the recorded conversations showed that the president knew about the illegal activities of CREEP. Many of the advisors resigned. Some were arrested. A few went to jail. Their crimes included burglary, conspiracy,[2] and obstruction of justice.[3]

7

Next, Congress[4] got ready to impeach the president. Nixon decided not to wait for impeachment. Instead, he became the first U.S. president to resign.

8

Many journalists dream about writing a story that changes the world. Woodward and Bernstein won a Pulitzer Prize for their investigation into Watergate. They wrote books about their story. One of the books, *All the President's Men*, was made into a Hollywood movie. The careful investigation by these two journalists is an unforgettable event in U.S. history: It led to the resignation of the 37th president of the United States.

9

---

[2] *conspiracy:* a plan by a group of people to secretly do something bad or illegal

[3] *obstruction of justice:* stopping the police or law courts from doing their job

[4] *Congress:* the elected group of people in the United States who are responsible for making laws; the Senate and the House of Representatives

4 READING CHECK

A Circle the letter of the name of the person or people described.

1 This person helped investigate the Watergate break-in.
   a George McGovern   **b** Richard Nixon   **c** Carl Bernstein

2 This person was the Democratic candidate for president in 1972.
   a George McGovern   **b** Richard Nixon   **c** Bob Woodward

3 This person won the 1972 presidential election.
   a George McGovern   **b** Richard Nixon   **c** Bob Woodward

4 These people won a journalism award for their reporting.
   a all the journalists at *The Washington Post*
   b Woodward and Bernstein
   c the investigators of the FBI

B Answer the questions with information from the reading.

1 Where is the Watergate Hotel located?

_____

2 There was a burglary in a room at the hotel. Who did the room belong to?

_____

3 What were some unusual details that the police had reported about the burglary?

_____

4 Who did one of the burglars work for?

_____

5 What did people close to President Nixon want *The Washington Post* to do?

_____

6 What did the FBI find out about President Nixon?

_____

7 What did Congress want to do to Nixon?

_____

8 What award did Woodward and Bernstein win?

_____

5 VOCABULARY CHECK

A Retell the story. Fill in the blanks with the correct words from the box.

article	campaigns	candidate	cover	evidence
headquarters	illegal	political parties	sources	term

In the last year of Richard Nixon's first _____ of
office as U.S. president, the two _____ , the Republicans
                              2
and Democrats, were running _____ for the new
                        3
presidential election. Nixon was running for re-election as the Republican

_____ .
            4

One day, two journalists, Bob Woodward and Carl Bernstein, decided to
_____ the story of a hotel burglary that had happened at
              5
the Democratic Party _____ . They learned that one of the
                             6
suspects had worked for Nixon. Then, they found many _____
                                                7
of information to help them write their _____ .
                                            8

Nixon won the election, but the FBI had found _____ that
                                            9
Nixon knew about the _____ activities. As a result, Congress
                        10
decided to impeach the president, but Nixon quickly resigned.

B Fill in the blanks with the correct words. Use the correct verb tense or the
correct singular or plural noun form.

Verb	Noun	Adjective
impeach	impeachment	impeached
investigate	investigation	investigative
publish	publisher	publishing
report	reporter	–
resign	resignation	–

1 The journalists _____ the crime before they wrote about it.

2 The newspaper won a major _____ award last year.

3 Some _____ work for television and some for newspapers.

4 The president faced _____ for his illegal activities.

5 The country was happy to accept the president's _____ .

6 APPLYING READING SKILLS

You will often read about how one event causes another event to happen.
***Finding causes and effects** in a reading can help you understand the reading better.*

A Match the cause on the left with its effect on the right.

1 _____	There was an unusual burglary at the Watergate Hotel.	**a** Congress started an impeachment trial to remove the president from office.
2 _____	The reporters published articles connecting the crime to the president's administration.	**b** Two reporters decided to cover the story.
3 _____	The FBI accused Nixon's advisors of illegal activities and learned that the president knew about them.	**c** The public became angry, and the FBI started an investigation.

B Find one effect in the text for each cause.

CAUSE	EFFECT
1 Some news sources told the reporters that their information was "off the record."	
2 The American Congress decided to impeach President Nixon.	
3 The FBI got involved in the investigation.	
4 Woodward and Bernstein did an excellent investigation of Watergate.	

7 DISCUSSION

Discuss the following questions in pairs or groups.

1 Do you think it is wrong to secretly record a conversation? Explain.
2 Do you agree that sources for news stories should be secret? Explain.
3 Can you think of any events that the media should not cover? Explain.

VOCABULARY REVIEW

Chapter **10**	Chapter **11**	Chapter **12**
Political Science	**Political Science**	**Political Science**
defeat (*v.*) · **govern** · (in) **power** · (have) **rights** · **take control**	**activist** · **democratically** · **dictator** · **elected** (*adj.*) · **resistance**	**campaign** (*n.*) · **candidate** · **headquarters** · **impeach** · **political party** · **resign** · **term** (of office)
Academic Word List	**Academic Word List**	**Academic Word List**
conflict (*n.*) · (on) **display** · **document** (*n.*) · **policy** · **principle** · **stability**	**affect** (*v.*) · **controversial** · **exhibit** (*v.*) · **liberate** · **reaction** · **symbol**	**evidence** · **illegal** · **investigate** · **publish** · **source**
History	**Art**	**Journalism**
conquer · **historian** · **kingdom** · **slave**	**canvas** · **inspired** (*adj.*) · **masterpiece** · **sensation**	**article** · **cover** (*v.*) · **report** (*v.*)

Find words in the chart that match the definitions. Answers to 1–4 are from Chapter 10. Answers to 5–8 are from Chapter 11. Answers to 9–12 are from Chapter 12.

1 When something is not likely to change or to move: _____

2 To cause another person or group to lose, so you can win: _____

3 A person owned by another person: _____

4 To make laws for an area, state, or country: _____

5 To influence someone or something; to cause change: _____

6 Filled with the desire to do something or create something: _____

7 The cloth an artist paints on: _____

8 Done in a way so that the people are represented: _____

9 Against the law: _____

10 A piece of writing in a newspaper or a magazine: _____

11 The main offices for a company or another official group: _____

12 To examine carefully; to try to find the truth: _____

VOCABULARY IN USE

Work with a partner or small group, and discuss the questions below.

1 If you were a **historian**, what historical time and place would you study?

2 What is the best way to end a **conflict** with a friend? Explain.

3 Why do leaders sometimes **resign** from a company or a political position?

4 What do you think is the most **controversial** topic in the news today? Explain.

5 What do you think makes a work of art a **masterpiece**? Explain.

6 What do you think would be a good **symbol** of peace? Explain.

7 If you could **publish** a book, what would it be about?

8 How many **terms of office** do you think the leader of a country should have? Explain.

ROLE PLAY

Work with a partner. One student is a candidate running for a political office. The other student is a newspaper reporter covering the campaign.

Reporter: Prepare general questions to ask the candidate about his or her policies and principles for leadership.

Candidate: Prepare a list of your policies and principles for leadership.

WRITING

Write a journal entry as if you were Cyrus the Great, Pablo Picasso, or Richard Nixon. As you write your entry, answer the following questions.

- What happened in your life today?

- How did the event make you feel?

- What did you do as a result of the event?

- What did you learn from the event?

WEBQUEST

Find more information about the topics in this unit by going on the Internet. Go to www.cambridge.org/readthis and follow the instructions for doing a WebQuest. Search for facts. Have fun. Good luck!

Automotive Technology

Chapter 13

Catching Crime Cars

Find that car! Solve that crime! You'll be surprised how often cars help the police solve crimes.

Content areas:
- Automotive Technology
- Criminal Justice

Chapter 14

The Most Dangerous Race

Every year, a race through wild and dangerous places pushes cars and drivers to their limits.

Content areas:
- Automotive Technology
- Geography

Chapter 15

Cars of the Future

The cars of the future might be here sooner than you think!

Content areas:
- Automotive Technology
- Industrial Design

13

Catching Crime Cars

1 TOPIC PREVIEW

A Write the number of the car part in the correct blank in the diagram. Share your answers with your classmates.

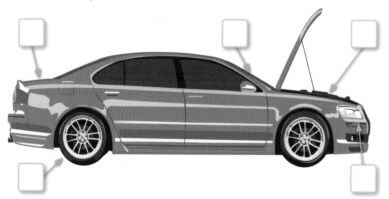

1 windshield
2 tire
3 headlight
4 engine
5 trunk

B Read the title of this chapter, look at the picture, and discuss the following questions.

1 What do you think a "crime car" is?
2 Do you think any of the car parts in Part A could help police solve a crime? Explain.
3 What do you think the reading is going to be about?

2 VOCABULARY PREVIEW

A Read the word lists. Put a check (✓) next to the words that you know and can use in a sentence. Compare your answers with a partner. Then look up any unfamiliar words in a dictionary.

Automotive Technology	Academic Word List	Criminal Justice
frame (*n.*)	**analysis**	**clue**
high-tech	**identification**	**confess**
(car) **model**	**require**	**crime scene**
(tire) **tread** (*n.*)	**transport**	**hit-and-run**
truck	**vehicle**	**stolen property**

The chart shows selected words from the reading related to automotive technology, criminal justice, and the Academic Word List (AWL). For more information about the AWL, see page 121.

B Fill in the blanks with words from Part A.

1 The accident was a/an _____ ; no one saw the driver.

2 Many colleges _____ new students to live on campus.

3 Dr. Lee works with the newest _____ equipment.

4 A driver's license is often used as a/an _____ card.

5 He bought a/an _____ with an open back to carry large items.

6 The child was afraid to _____ that she stole the candy.

7 A sample of blood was sent to the laboratory for _____ .

8 The police put yellow tape around the _____ to keep people out.

9 A car is one type of _____ .

10 The _____ gives a car its basic shape, so it has to be very strong.

11 One _____ that led police to the criminal was a bit of his hair.

12 Big ships _____ products from one country to another.

13 The police found _____ , such as jewelry and TVs, in the house.

14 The automobile company started making a new _____ of car.

15 The tire _____ left deep marks in the mud.

Preview the questions in Reading Check Part A on page 102. Then read the story.

Catching Crime Cars

1   It was a case of hit-and-run. A speeding car struck and badly injured a boy on a bicycle. Instead of stopping to help, the car's driver sped away and disappeared. The police in the Canadian city of Sudbury, where the accident occurred, had very few clues. No one had seen the accident. How could they find the driver?

2   The car was the key. On the boy's clothing was a small bit of paint, probably from the car that hit him. Scientific analysis showed that the paint might have come from a certain model of car, a Chrysler Coronet. The police examined hundreds of Coronets, but the paint from the crime scene didn't match any of them. Finally, officers found an old car with paint that matched perfectly. Government records showed who had owned the car, and the police caught the guilty driver.

3   Cars are involved in many crimes. As in the Sudbury case, the car might have hit someone or something. In other cases, cars transport criminals, weapons, stolen property, or even crime victims to or from the location of a crime. Just as a criminal leaves behind fingerprints,[1] hair, or footprints, crime cars leave signs saying, "I was here."

---

[1] *fingerprints:* marks made on an object by the patterns of curved lines at the ends of fingers and thumbs

The signs pointing to a crime car are called "trace evidence."[2] In addition to paint, trace evidence may be a tire track, a piece of glass, a spot of oil, a piece of metal, or even a whole part from a car. Crime scene investigators (CSIs) take pictures of the scene and carefully collect objects, hoping that something might hold an important clue.

4

In one case, a car full of explosives blew up under a New York City building. The explosion caused a lot of damage and destroyed most evidence that could point to the driver. Among the twisted metal and broken glass, however, CSIs found part of a car's frame. It had a vehicle identification number on it. Police records matched the number with a car owned by a car-rental company in New Jersey. The police quickly arrested the man who had rented the car.

5

Tire tracks can also be especially useful. Every tire has an easy-to-see tread, a pattern of lines in the rubber. Even without special equipment, police can often see this pattern in mud, on grass, or even on the surface of a hard road near a crime scene. A case in the state of Minnesota is a good example. The police tried for four years to find a criminal who had set several forest fires. Then they found an old tire track, obviously from a truck, at the edge of a burned-out forest. An officer took a picture and tried to match the tread pattern to the tires of trucks he saw around town. Finally, he found a perfect match, and the truck's owner confessed to starting the fires.

6

Most trace evidence is harder to analyze. It must be sent to crime laboratories, where high-tech equipment can identify it. For example, a laboratory may analyze broken window glass from a crime scene. How does it bend light that shines into it? What chemicals is it made of? With a report from the lab, a CSI can search a computer database for car models that have the right kind of glass. Only a few models will match. The police may not have found the exact crime car, but they will know what kinds to look for.

7

Databases matching car models to paint, glass, or other evidence get better every year. Still, CSIs have a tough job. Millions and millions of cars have been manufactured. Many cars have been destroyed. Others are not on the streets, but parked in garages. Finding that one car used in a crime will therefore always require not just science, but also quite a bit of luck.

8

---

[2] *trace evidence:* a small amount of evidence

4 READING CHECK

A Are these statements true or false? Write *T* (true) or *F* (false).

1 _____ Crime cars are only involved in traffic accidents.

2 _____ Crime cars can leave "trace evidence" at a crime scene.

3 _____ Crime Scene Investigators (CSIs) don't need special equipment to analyze trace evidence.

B Circle the letter of the best answer.

1 Why do the police try to find crime cars?
   a to find criminals   **b** to find trace evidence   **c** to find car models

2 Who was the victim of the hit-and-run in the Canadian city of Sudbury?
   a a car driver   **b** a bicycle rider   **c** a police officer

3 What evidence helped the police solve the Sudbury case?
   a a bit of paint   **b** the boy's hair   **c** broken glass

4 How did CSIs find the person who left a car to explode under a New York City building?
   a They matched bits of paint to his car.
   b An identification number matched with a car he had rented.
   c A car-rental place called the police and identified him.

5 How did the police officer in Minnesota match tire tracks to a truck in the town?
   a by finding tires in a database
   b by sending tire tracks to a lab
   c by comparing a photograph of tire tracks to tires

6 Why are tire treads especially useful in catching crime cars?
   a They can lead CSIs to one or two car models.
   b They leave identification numbers at every crime scene.
   c CSIs can see their patterns without special equipment.

7 What is true about high-tech equipment?
   a It can find things that are not easy for CSIs to see.
   b It is used only to analyze pieces of glass.
   c CSIs don't need it if they have good databases.

8 What effect will better databases have?
   a CSIs will not need to be lucky.
   b CSIs will be able to match evidence to car models more easily.
   c CSIs will no longer use trace evidence to find crime cars.

5 VOCABULARY CHECK

A Retell the story. Fill in the blanks with the correct words from the box.

analysis	clues	crime scene	high-tech	hit-and-run
identification	model	require	treads	vehicle

Cars involved in crimes leave behind _____ that can help police find criminals. For example, in a/an _____ case, some paint from a crime car was found on the victim. Other evidence found at a/an _____ could include glass, oil, or tracks from the _____ of tires. Sometimes, a whole part from a/an _____ is found. This part might have a/an _____ number on it. Crime scene investigators (CSIs) often _____ help from a crime lab. _____ equipment in the lab can often match a piece of evidence with a/an _____ of car. This _____ then makes it easier for CSIs to catch the criminals.

B Circle the best word or words to complete each sentence.

1 The man wanted to (confess / identify / release) his crime to the police.

2 The (tire tread / frame / evidence) of the car was made out of metal.

3 (A tire tread / Stolen property / A landmark) was found in the trunk of the car.

4 Crime cars sometimes (send / transport / match) weapons to crime scenes.

5 Tire tread patterns on the road gave police clues to find the (boat / truck / jewelry).

6 APPLYING READING SKILLS

Finding main ideas is a key reading skill. Each paragraph in a reading usually has a main idea. When you can find each main idea and summarize it, you know that you have understood the most important parts of a reading.

A Look back at the reading. Find the paragraph number that matches the one-sentence summary containing the main idea of the paragraph.

PARAGRAPH	ONE-SENTENCE MAIN IDEA SUMMARY
	Cars are involved in many different types of crimes.
	A small piece of a destroyed car can lead to its identity.
	Databases for cars are improving, but luck is still needed to find a crime car.
	A hit-and-run case left very few clues.

B Write a one-sentence summary for each of the other four paragraphs in the reading. Compare your summaries with a partner.

PARAGRAPH	ONE-SENTENCE MAIN IDEA SUMMARY

7 DISCUSSION

Discuss the following questions in pairs or groups.

1 Have you ever seen CSIs catch crime cars in movies or on television? Did they use any of the methods in the reading? Explain.

2 Could companies that make cars help in the search for crime cars? If so, how?

3 Is car theft a problem in your community? If so, how do people try to prevent it?

CHAPTER 14
The Most Dangerous Race

1 TOPIC PREVIEW

A Imagine that you are in a car race and have to drive through these difficult places. What would you need in each place? Write one or two things you would need. Share your answers with your classmates.

1 a desert: _____

2 high mountains: _____

3 rocky places: _____

4 rivers: _____

5 a rain forest: _____

B Read the title of this chapter, look at the picture, and discuss the following questions.

1 Have you ever seen a car race? Did it look dangerous? Explain.

2 What does the picture show? Describe it.

3 What do you think the reading is going to be about?

2 VOCABULARY PREVIEW

A Read the word lists. Put a check (✓) next to the words that you know and can use in a sentence. Compare your answers with a partner. Then look up any unfamiliar words in a dictionary.

Automotive Technology	Academic Word List	Geography
break down (*v.*) install motorcycle shock absorber	adjust concentrate (on) maximum route	cliff continent desert landmark navigate sandstorm terrain

The chart shows selected words from the reading related to automotive technology, geography, and the Academic Word List (AWL). For more information about the AWL, see page 121.

B Write the word from Part A next to its definition.

1 To find a way to get from one place to another: _____

2 To put equipment somewhere and make it ready to use: _____

3 A vehicle with a motor and two wheels: _____

4 A certain kind of land (rocky, dry, etc.): _____

5 The way from one place to another: _____

6 A part of a car that prevents passengers from bouncing: _____

7 An extremely hot, dry place: _____

8 One of the seven large areas of land on Earth: _____

9 To change something slightly and make it more effective:

_____

10 Something caused by a strong wind in a hot, dry place: _____

11 A hillside that drops sharply, almost straight down: _____

12 The most: _____

13 Something that helps you recognize where you are: _____

14 To think very carefully about something you are doing: _____

15 To stop working; usually used to describe a machine: _____

3 READING

Preview the questions in Reading Check Part A on page 109. Then read the story.

The Most Dangerous Race

Car crash at the Dakar Rally

The Dakar Rally, a long and dangerous race, is famous for breaking both humans and machines. One driver rolled his car down a cliff and broke his shoulder. Another drove through a war zone where a bomb exploded under his car. Others have been buried in sand, swept away by rivers, shot at, or lost for days.

The first Dakar Rally was organized by French driver Thierry Sabine. After driving through the harsh conditions of Africa's Sahara Desert in 1977, Sabine decided that car races should include adventure and danger. In December 1978, Sabine and drivers for 182 cars and motorcycles gathered for the first rally. They began the race in central Paris and traveled through the Sahara to Dakar, Senegal, in West Africa. The drivers faced more than 6,000 miles (almost 10,000 kilometers) of mountains, sandstorms, and snakes. Most of the racers crashed, got lost, or dropped out because their vehicles broke down. Only 74 cars and motorcycles reached Dakar on January 14, 1979.

The Dakar route changes every year but always goes through some of Earth's deadliest terrain. Navigating through this terrain is a big challenge. The race lasts more than two weeks and is divided into one-day sections. Each evening, officials hand out road books for the next day's section. The book gives only general information, such as the day's destination, places to pass along the way, some basic directions, and warnings about danger spots. The driver and his or her team have to figure out how to get to the destination. Detailed maps and normal

GPS[1] systems are not allowed. The driver concentrates on going as fast as possible. Meanwhile, a navigator in the passenger seat looks for landmarks, such as hills or unusual rocks, and chooses a route. Most landmarks are not in the road book, so a navigator has to rely on experience and make good guesses.

4   Getting lost is serious. In 1982, a driver named Mark Thatcher disappeared in the Sahara after his car broke down about 25 miles (about 40 km) off the route. Rescuers were pressured to find him fast because Thatcher was the son of Britain's prime minister. Six days later, a search team found him and his two teammates. They were still alive but very thirsty.

5   At first, all Dakar's cars were "production" vehicles, models that an ordinary person could buy at a car dealership.[2] Now, the Dakar is divided into groups for many different kinds of vehicles. One group is still only for production cars, most of which are familiar SUVs.[3] Teams are allowed to make a few changes to the cars, but production vehicles may not be turned into super-cars. They must still be basically like the cars available at the local Honda or Ford or Volkswagen dealership. Most changes that are allowed relate to the tough Dakar terrain. Some teams put in strong shock absorbers for rocky ground or strong rubber around doors and windows to keep out desert sand. Teams may adjust engines to get maximum power in thin mountain air. Most drivers install a system to control air pressure in the tires by simply pushing a button.

6   In 2008, armed rebels[4] in Mauritania threatened to kill or kidnap racers, so an African route became too dangerous even for the Dakar Rally. Therefore, in 2009, the race moved to another continent, South America. Racers bounced over sharp rock in Argentina and got stuck in Chile's Atacama Desert, the driest place on Earth. They drove twice across the Andes Mountains at about 10,000 feet (3,000 meters) above sea level. At those heights, drivers and car engines both struggled to get enough oxygen. Even in its new home, the Dakar Rally still beat about half of the racers. In 2009, 178 cars started the race, and only 91 crossed the finish line.

---

[1] *GPS:* Global Positioning System, in which satellite signals show your location and possible roads to take

[2] *car dealership:* a place that buys and sells automobiles

[3] *SUV:* Sport Utility Vehicle; a very strong car that can travel over rough country

[4] *armed rebel:* a person who fights with guns or other weapons against the government or rulers

4 READING CHECK

A Are these statements true or false? Write *T* (true) or *F* (false).

1 _____ The Dakar Rally goes through more than one country.

2 _____ Race officials tell drivers exactly which roads to take.

3 _____ Dakar drivers often get hurt or lost.

B Circle the letter of the best answer.

1 Why did Thierry Sabine set the Dakar course through the desert?
   a He was born in Africa.
   b Driving through cities was too dangerous.
   c He thought car races should involve adventure and danger.

2 How long is each section of the Dakar Rally?
   a one day   **b** about two weeks   **c** one year

3 What information is *not* in a road book?
   a the destination
   b warnings about danger spots
   c how to reach the destination

4 Why were rescuers under a lot of pressure to find Mark Thatcher fast?
   a He was the son of an important person.
   b He had been winning the race.
   c He had been kidnapped by armed rebels.

5 How is a production vehicle different from other vehicles?
   a It can go through rough territory.
   b It breaks down a lot during the race.
   c It is a model that ordinary people can buy.

6 Why do Dakar drivers make changes to a car's shock absorbers?
   a so the driver will not get lost
   b so the car will work better in rough country
   c so the car will be easier to sell in dealerships

7 Why did the Dakar Rally move to South America in 2009?
   a because drivers might get killed if they went through Africa
   b because the route through Africa was no longer rough enough
   c because drivers knew the African route too well

8 Which of the following was *not* part of the 2009 Dakar route?
   a Mauritania   **b** Argentina   **c** Chile

5 VOCABULARY CHECK

A Retell the story. Fill in the blanks with the correct words from the box.

cliff	continent	desert	landmarks
maximum	motorcycles	route	sandstorms
shock absorbers	terrain		

The Dakar Rally is a race through some of the roughest

_____ on Earth. The first race started in Paris, went

1

through the Sahara _____ in Africa, and ended in Dakar,

2

Senegal. Since then, the _____ has often changed, but

3

racers have always faced dangers along the way. They don't have detailed

maps, so they have to find their way by spotting _____

4

and guessing which way to go. If they go the wrong way, they could get lost,

roll down a _____ , or even drive into a war zone. Bad

5

weather like _____ or flooding rain may strike.

6

The race now includes not only cars and _____ but other

7

kinds of vehicles. Drivers can put in extra-strong _____

8

and make other changes so their cars can handle the rough country. In

2009, the race moved to the _____ of South America to

9

avoid wars in Africa. Still, the Dakar Rally demands _____

10

effort from drivers, who still face some of the worst places on Earth.

B Circle the word that does not fit. Use a dictionary if necessary.

1	Things people **adjust**:	an engine	a radio	a hill
2	Things that can **break down**:	a system	a car	a river
3	Things people **navigate**:	roads	seas	drivers
4	Things people **install**:	air conditioners	danger	tires
5	Things a racer **concentrates** on:	directions	sea level	speed

6 APPLYING READING SKILLS

*In a reading, some ideas are not stated directly. **Making inferences** means using logic to discover what these ideas are.*

A The following facts are stated in the reading. Match each fact with an inference that you can make.

FACT	INFERENCE
1 _____ In 2009, 178 cars started the race and only 91 cars finished it.	**a** The idea of the race was to test how ordinary people in ordinary cars could do in difficult terrain.
2 _____ In the first Dakar races, only regular production cars were used.	**b** To make navigation more challenging, drivers cannot use the latest technology.
3 _____ Racers do not have normal GPS systems.	**c** During the race, some cars broke down, some racers got sick, and some racers got lost.

B Put a check (✓) next to each statement that is an inference you can make from the reading. Explain your choices to a partner.

1 _____ Some drivers in the first Dakar Rally probably died during the race.

2 _____ Thierry Sabine considered the Sahara Desert a dangerous place.

3 _____ Some drivers in the Dakar Rally are women.

4 _____ Sometimes navigators drive for a while so the drivers can rest.

5 _____ Some racing teams can be removed from the race for making too many changes to their cars.

6 _____ Bicycles made for rough terrain can enter the Dakar Rally.

7 DISCUSSION

Discuss the following questions in pairs or groups.

1 Would you like to be in the Dakar Rally? Why or why not?

2 Do you think Dakar drivers should be allowed to use new technology? Explain.

3 If you could create an exciting race that would involve adventure and danger, what would your race be like? Explain.

1 TOPIC PREVIEW

A Imagine yourself 50 years in the future. Put a check (✓) next to the vehicles below that you might see at that time. Share your answers with your classmates.

1 _____ a flying bicycle

2 _____ a car that floats on water

3 _____ a backpack with a jet on it that allows a person to fly

4 _____ a car that doesn't need gas or electricity

5 _____ _____ (your idea)

B Read the title of this chapter, look at the picture, and discuss the following questions.

1 What would you like to see in cars of the future?

2 Describe the vehicles in the picture. What are their unique features?

3 What do you think the reading is going to be about?

2 Vocabulary Preview

A Read the word lists. Put a check (✓) next to the words that you know and can use in a sentence. Compare your answers with a partner. Then look up any unfamiliar words in a dictionary.

Automotive Technology	Academic Word List	Industrial Design
drag (*n.*) fuel-efficient hybrid (*adj.*) run on (*v.*)	evolve generation shift (in) (*n.*) style (*n.*) transition	aerodynamic curve (*n.*) cutting-edge (*adj.*) futuristic old-fashioned prototype

The chart shows selected words from the reading related to automotive technology, industrial design, and the Academic Word List (AWL). For more information about the AWL, see page 121.

B Fill in the blanks with words from Part A.

1 She's a first-_____ Canadian; her parents came from China.

2 The doctor uses the most _____ technology to help her patients.

3 The _____ caused by the high winds made the car move slowly.

4 Most cars _____ unleaded gasoline.

5 Big cars use a lot of gas. They are not _____ .

6 The history museum displayed _____ clothes from the 1920s.

7 The movie was a/an _____ film about life in the next century.

8 Starting a new job can be a difficult _____ for many people.

9 A product takes years to _____ from an idea to its completion.

10 His new _____ car runs on both electricity and gasoline.

11 Please drive slowly! There is a/an _____ in the road ahead.

12 There has been a/an _____ in thinking toward saving energy.

13 The _____ shape of a bird and its wings helps the bird to fly.

14 The designers built a/an _____ of a new electric car.

15 I like that designer's modern _____ of clothing.

Preview the questions in Reading Check Part A on page 116. Then read the story.

Cars of the Future

boxfish (inset image); The Mercedes Bionic

1   It's five o'clock, and you've finished work for the day. You exit your office building and cross the parking lot to your vehicle. Its bright green paint and aerodynamic curves make it look more like a colorful tropical fish than a car. As you drive home, you look up and see several flying cars move through the air above the crowded highway. Suddenly, a triangle-shaped, three-wheeled vehicle passes you. While this scene seems like something out of a science-fiction[1] film, this is the future of cars. These cars may be here sooner than you think.

2   The idea of flying an automobile to escape highway traffic is a driver's dream. This is not a new idea. Over the past 90 years, there have been at least 104 "flying cars," but none have succeeded. One company, Terrafugia, however, has successfully invented the first roadable[2] aircraft called the Transition. The Transition works because it both flies in the air like an airplane and drives on the ground like a car. It has an aircraft engine but runs on automotive gasoline. It has two seats and folding wings. The Transition can change from a car to an airplane in 15 seconds. Though it is unlikely that the Transition will be seen in the near future, it's exciting to know that modern ideas may soon change the way cars are built.

---

[1] *science fiction:* stories or films which are about science or technology of the future
[2] *roadable:* a vehicle that can be operated on a road

Another vehicle we may see in the future is the XR3. The XR3   3
is a three-wheeled vehicle shaped like a triangle. The point of the
triangle rests over the single rear wheel. Its unique shape and shiny
silver exterior give the car a futuristic style. What makes the XR3 so
different is that it can be built at home, and you don't have to be an
automotive expert to build it. Clear instructions and materials can be
bought from the designer. Known as a "personal transit vehicle," the
XR3 holds one person. It's a hybrid car that runs on both electricity
and gas and gets 125 miles (201 kilometers) per gallon (3.8 liters). The
XR3 is designed for people who want to save fuel and build their own
vehicle. For this reason, the designer is confident that the XR3 is the
car of the future.

The car company Mercedes has developed a car called the Bionic,   4
modeled after a tropical fish, the boxfish. The cutting-edge design
is a result of the company's effort to make a more fuel-efficient car.
One reason some cars waste gas is that they produce too much drag.
Drag is the resistance an object feels when it moves through the air
or water. The higher the drag on a car, the more fuel it takes to move
the car. The streamlined boxfish produces little drag as it moves
through the water. The Bionic imitates the aerodynamic shape of the
boxfish and uses twenty percent less fuel than today's standard cars.
This helps the Bionic's engine get 70 miles per gallon. Mercedes does
not plan on making the car available to the public in the near future.
However, the Bionic shows us that by using nature as a guide, cars can
be extremely fuel-efficient.

While these three vehicles may only be prototypes now, they inspire   5
the next generation of cars. In the twenty-first century, we have
already seen a shift in car design. It's not uncommon to see hybrid
electric cars on the road. Cars that run on alternative fuel sources,
such as liquid natural gas, ethanol[3] and biodiesel[4] are also becoming
more popular. As car designs continue to evolve, we may soon see
vehicles like the Transition, the XR3, and the Bionic on the road – or
in the air. Perhaps one day in the future, you'll fly in a car with your
grandchild to an automobile museum. You'll both be amazed at the
old-fashioned cars that we drive today.

---

[3] *ethanol:* an automobile fuel made from corn or grain and combined with gasoline
[4] *biodiesel:* an automobile fuel made from vegetable oil or animal fat and combined
        with petroleum diesel

4 READING CHECK

A Circle the letter of the best answer.

1 What is the main advantage of the car called the Transition?
   a It can float in the water.
   b It can fly above traffic.
   c It can hold many passengers.

2 What is the main advantage of the car called the XR3?
   a It can get up to 150 miles per gallon.
   b It is inexpensive.
   c It runs on both electricity and gas.

3 What is the main advantage of the car called the Bionic?
   a It is both a car and a boat.
   b It is fuel-efficient.
   c It can get up to 170 miles per gallon.

B Answer the questions with information from the reading.

1 What does the Transition look like?

_____

2 Why did the company Terrafugia name its vehicle the Transition?

_____

3 What does the XR3 look like?

_____

4 Why is the XR3 different from other cars?

_____

5 What is one reason some cars waste gas?

_____

6 How much fuel does the Bionic save compared to other cars?

_____

7 What kinds of cars are becoming popular today?

_____

5 VOCABULARY CHECK

A Retell the story. Fill in the blanks with the correct words from the box.

aerodynamic	curves	cutting-edge	drag	fuel-efficient
futuristic	generation	hybrid	runs on	shift

Cars of the future may be here sooner than you think. There has already been a/an _____ in car design in the twenty-first century, and a new _____ of cars is being designed today. The Transition is the first successful vehicle that can change from a car to an airplane. It _____ automotive gasoline. The XR3 looks like a/an _____ car because of its unusual triangular shape and shiny exterior. It is a/an _____ car that uses both gasoline and electricity. The Mercedes Bionic is a car modeled after a boxfish. The boxfish has a/an _____ shape, so it does not produce much _____ as it moves through the water. The Bionic's fishlike _____ not only make it _____ , but they also give the car a/an _____ design. It's exciting to think that one of these three vehicles could be in your future!

B Circle the best word to complete each sentence.

1 The engineer will plan the (style / transition / drag) from producing a gas-powered car to an electric one.

2 You are (futuristic / cutting-edge / old-fashioned) if you don't like new technology.

3 She preferred a conservative (generation / style / method) of clothing.

4 The product you see on store shelves was probably based on a (prototype / style / curve).

5 Computers have (styled / evolved / come) from very large machines to tiny, hand-held ones.

6 APPLYING READING SKILLS

Your reading speed is the number of words you can read per minute.
Increasing your reading speed *will make it easier to do all the reading for your classes. Timing yourself when you read will help you read faster.*

A Reread "Cars of the Future" on page 114, and time yourself. Write your starting time, your finishing time, and the number of minutes it took you to read. Then calculate your reading speed.

> **Story title:** "Cars of the Future" (639 words)
> Starting time: _____
> Finishing time: _____
> Total reading time: _____ minutes
> *Reading speed: _____ words per minute

*To calculate your reading speed, divide the number of words in the text (639) by your total reading time (the number of minutes you needed to read the text).

B Now reread either "Catching Crime Cars" (634 words) on page 100 or "The Most Dangerous Race" (636 words) on page 107. Time yourself. Write the title of the story and your times below. Then calculate your reading speed.

> **Story title:** _____ (_____ words)
> Starting time: _____
> Finishing time: _____
> Total reading time: _____ minutes
> Reading speed: _____ words per minute

7 DISCUSSION

Discuss the following questions in pairs or groups.

1 Would you want to buy or drive the Transition, the XR3, or the Bionic? Explain.
2 Which car do you think would be the most popular? Explain.
3 What forms of transportation do you think there will be 150 years from now? Explain.

VOCABULARY REVIEW

Chapter **13**	Chapter **14**	Chapter **15**
Automotive Technology	**Automotive Technology**	**Automotive Technology**
frame (*n.*) · high-tech · (car) model · (tire) tread (*n.*) · truck	break down (*v.*) · install · motorcycle · shock absorber	drag (*n.*) · fuel-efficient · hybrid (*adj.*) · run on (*v.*)
Academic Word List	**Academic Word List**	**Academic Word List**
analysis · identification · require · transport · vehicle	adjust · concentrate (on) · maximum · route	evolve · generation · shift (in) (*n.*) · style (*n.*) · transition
Criminal Justice	**Geography**	**Industrial Design**
clue · confess · crime scene · hit-and-run · stolen property	cliff · continent · desert · landmark · navigate · sandstorm · terrain	aerodynamic · curve (*n.*) · cutting-edge (*adj.*) · futuristic · old-fashioned · prototype

Find words in the chart that match the definitions. Answers to 1–4 are from Chapter 13. Answers to 5–8 are from Chapter 14. Answers to 9–12 are from Chapter 15.

1 A careful examination of something to understand it better: _____

2 The basic structure of a building, vehicle, or other object: _____

3 To admit that you have done something wrong: _____

4 An object or information that helps solve a crime: _____

5 To put equipment somewhere and make it ready to use: _____

6 To find a way to get from one place to another: _____

7 To stop working, usually used to describe a machine: _____

8 To think very carefully about something that you are doing: _____

9 The force of air that pushes against something as it moves: _____

10 To change gradually over a long period of time: _____

11 Very modern and with all the newest developments: _____

12 A particular design or fashion for something: _____

VOCABULARY IN USE

Work with a partner or small group, and discuss the questions below.

1 Do you think everyone should carry **identification** cards? Explain.

2 Should there be a **maximum** age to obtain a driver's license? Explain.

3 Why is it important for police to keep people out of a **crime scene**?

4 Do you think **motorcycle** riders should wear a helmet? Explain.

5 What are some famous **landmarks** in your country? Why are they famous?

6 Do you have any **old-fashioned** products that you still use today? Explain.

7 What are some differences between your **generation** and your parents' generation?

8 If you could travel to any **continent**, which one would you travel to?

ROLE PLAY

Work with a partner. Student A is a newspaper reporter. Student B is one of the following:

- **a crime scene investigator (CSI)**

- **a Dakar Rally navigator**

- **a car designer**

Student A: Prepare general questions to ask Student B about the personal characteristics and other requirements for his or her job. Additionally, prepare questions to ask about what Student B likes and dislikes about the job.

Student B: Prepare a list of the personal characteristics and other requirements necessary for your job. Additionally, prepare a list of things you like or dislike about the job.

WRITING

Write a newspaper article about one of the people above. You can use notes from your role play and other ideas.

WEBQUEST

Find more information about the topics in this unit by going on the Internet. Go to www.cambridge.org/readthis and follow the instructions for doing a WebQuest. Search for facts. Have fun. Good luck!

The Academic Word List

What are the most common words in academic English? Which words appear most frequently in readings in different academic subject areas? Dr. Averil Coxhead, who is currently a Senior Lecturer at Victoria University of Wellington in New Zealand, did research to try to answer these questions. The result was the Academic Word List (AWL).

Coxhead studied readings in English from many different academic fields. She found 570 words or word families that appear in many of those readings. These are words like *estimate* and *estimation*; *analyze, analysis,* and *analytical*; *evident, evidence,* and *evidently* – words that you can expect to find when reading a sociology text, a computer science text, or even a music studies text. So if you want to read nonfiction in English or academic English, these are the words that are going to be most useful for you to study and learn.

When you study the readings in *Read This!*, you will study words that belong to two different academic subject areas. These words will help you understand the topic of each reading. In addition, you will study AWL words in the readings. Learning the AWL words will help you, not just when you are reading on that topic, but when you read any academic text, because these words are likely to come up in your reading again and again.

In the list below, we show you all the words that are from the Academic Word List that are in all three books of the *Read This!* series. Many of these words appear in several of the readings. However, the words in the list that are followed by letters and numbers are words that are the focus of study in one of the readings. The letters and numbers show which book and chapter the word appears in. For example, "access RT2, 13" tells you that you study the word *access* in *Read This!* Book 2, Chapter 13. When the letters and numbers after the word appear in color, that tells you that the word is the focus of study in this *Read This!* book.

From time to time you might want to study the words in this list and test yourself. By going to the chapter where the word appears, you can see the words in context, which is one of the best ways to study new or unfamiliar words.

The following list shows the AWL words that appear in the *Read This!* series.

A

access RT2, 13
accurate
accurately RT2, 6
achieve
achievement RT1, 5
adjust RT3, 14
adult RT2, 12
affect RT3, 11
alternative
analysis RT2, 12; RT3, 13
analyze
appreciate RT3, 1
approach RT3, 1
approaching
approximately RT1, 13
area RT1, 3
assist RT2, 5
assistance
authority RT2, 13
available
aware
awareness RT3, 8

B

beneficial
benefit RT2, 9

C

challenge RT1, 7; RT2, 2;
    RT3, 3
challenged
challenging RT2, 14
channel
chapter

chemical RT3, 5
civil
classical
coincidence RT1, 9
collapse RT2, 13
comment
commit
communicate RT1, 1
communication
compensation
complex RT3, 4
computer
concentrate RT3, 14
concentration RT2, 14
conduct
conflict RT3, 10
constant
construct RT3, 1
construction
consultant
consume RT2, 9
contact RT3, 4
contrast
contribute
contribution RT1, 7
controversial RT3, 11
conventional RT3, 7
couple
create RT1, 3
creative RT2, 4
crucial RT2, 15
cultural
culture
cycle RT3, 6

D

data RT2, 9
define
design RT1, 14; RT3, 3
designer
detect RT2, 6
device RT3, 9
discriminate
discrimination
display RT3, 10
disposable RT3, 5
distinct RT3, 2
distinction
distinctive
distinctly
diverse RT3, 2
document RT3, 10
documented
domain

E

energy RT1, 15
enormous RT1, 10
environment
environmental
environmentally
equipment RT3, 8
establish RT3, 6
estate
estimate RT2, 13
eventually
evidence RT2, 12; RT3, 12
evolve RT3, 15
exhibit RT3, 11

expand RT2, 7

expert RT1, 2; RT2, 10; RT3, 5

export RT1, 12

F

feature RT1, 8

federal

federations

fee

file RT1, 5

final

finally

flexibility RT3, 9

flexible

focus RT1, 6

foundation RT3, 3

function RT1, 8

G

generation RT2, 13; RT3, 15

global RT1, 10

goal RT3, 8

grade

guideline RT1, 8

H

highlight

I

identical RT2, 11

identification RT3, 13

identified

identify RT2, 6

identifying

identity RT2, 10

illegal RT3, 12

image RT2, 4

impact RT2, 15

individual RT3, 7

injure

injured

injury RT3, 9

institute RT2, 4

instructions

intelligence

intelligent

intense RT3, 6

interaction RT3, 2

interactive

investigate RT2, 11; RT3, 12

investigating

investigation

investigative

investigator

investor

involve

isolate RT2, 8

issue

item

J

job

L

layer RT3, 3

legal

liberate RT3, 11

locate

location

M

maintain RT2, 5

major

maximum RT3, 14

media

medical

mental RT2, 14; RT3, 8

method RT2, 2

military

monitor RT3, 4

N

network RT1, 5

normal RT2, 3

normally RT1, 1

O

obviously RT2, 10

occur RT2, 8

option RT2, 15

P

participate RT1, 4

participation RT3, 7

partner RT1, 2

percent

period

philosophy

physical RT2, 8; RT3, 8

physically

policy RT3, 10

positive

predict RT1, 11; RT2, 6; RT3, 1

prime

principle RT3, 10

procedure RT2, 3

process RT2, 9; RT3, 5

project RT1, 5; RT3, 3

promote

psychological

psychologist

psychology

publish RT3, 12

publisher RT1, 4

publishing

purchase

R

range

ratio RT1, 8

reaction RT3, 11

recover RT2, 3

recovered

recovery RT3, 9

region RT3, 5

register RT1, 11

registration

relax

release RT3, 4

reluctant RT3, 2

rely

remove

require RT3, 13

research RT1, 1

researcher RT2, 1

resource

respond RT1, 7; RT2, 8

response

restrict RT2, 9

restricted

restricting

restriction

reveal RT3, 5

role RT2, 13

route RT3, 14

S

section

security RT1, 2

sequence RT1, 9

shift RT3, 15

significant RT3, 2

significantly RT2, 9

similar RT2, 1

similarity RT1, 9

site RT2, 6

source RT1, 15; RT2, 7; RT3, 12

specific RT1, 14

specifically RT3, 9

specification

specify

stability RT3, 10

stabilize

stable

strategy RT1, 12

stress RT2, 14

structure RT1, 13; RT2, 4; RT3, 3

style RT1, 4; RT3, 15

survey RT3, 4

survive RT2, 3; RT3, 6

survivor

sustainable

symbol RT1, 3; RT2, 7; RT3, 11

T

tape RT1, 6

task

team

technology

theory RT2, 2

trace

tradition

traditional RT3, 2

traditionally

transit

transition RT3, 15

transport RT2, 5; RT3, 13

U

uniform

unique RT1, 14; RT2, 11; RT3, 1

V

vehicle RT3, 13

virtual

volunteer RT1, 15

Art Credits

1 *(left to right)* ©Kai Tirkkonen/Getty Images; ©Courtesy of The Travel Channel; ©Air View Online
2 ©Kai Tirkkonen/Getty Images
4 ©Jorma Luhta/Nature Picture Library
9 ©Courtesy of The Travel Channel
11 ©Courtesy of The Travel Channel
16 ©Air View Online
18 ©Avatra images/Alamy
25 *(left to right)* ©Tsuneo Nakamura/Photo Library; ©Dimitar Dilkoff/Getty Images; ©Leanna Rathkelly/Getty Images
26 ©Tsuneo Nakamura/Photo Library
28 ©Courtesy of Jamstec
33 ©Dimitar Dilkoff/Getty Images
40 ©Leanna Rathkelly/Getty Images
42 *(left to right)* ©Courtesy of U.S. Forestry service; ©Courtesy of Bailey's, Inc.
49 *(left to right)* ©AFP/Getty Images; ©Courtesy of Amazon Swim; ©Phil Cole/Getty Images
50 ©AFP/Getty Images
52 *(left to right)* ©Popperfoto/Getty Images; ©Greg Wood/Getty Images
57 ©Courtesy of Amazon Swim
59 ©Courtesy of Amazon Swim
64 ©Phil Cole/Getty Images
66 ©Alberto Ramella/AP Wide World Photo
73 *(left to right)* ©North Wind Picture Archives; ©Hemis/Alamy; ©Harry Ransom Center/University of Texas at Austin
74 ©North Wind Picture Archives
76 ©The British Museum
77 ©The British Museum
81 ©Hemis/Alamy
83 ©Interfoto/Alamy
88 ©Harry Ransom Center/University of Texas at Austin
90 ©AP Wide World Photo
97 *(left to right)* ©Robert J. Bennett/Photo Library; ©Eric Vargiolu/DPPI; ©Courtesy of Terrafugia
98 ©Robert J. Bennett/Photo Library
100 ©Pablo Paul/Alamy
105 ©Eric Vargiolu/DPPI
107 ©Gabriel Bouys/Getty Images
112 ©Courtesy of Terrafugia
114 *(fish)* ©Michael Stubblefield/Alamy; *(car)* ©Courtesy of Daimler AG